Career Track or Side Track

A Career Guide for Young African American Professionals

By Lionel Butler

Career Track or Side Track
A Career Guide for Young African-American Professionals

First Printing July 2001

Published by Class Life Publishing
Post Office Box 750593
Houston, Texas 77275-0593

For additional copies call Class Life Publishing
(281) 484-4753
Cover artwork by Volume Media, Inc.

ISBN: 0-9707568-0-1
Library of Congress Control Number: 2001012345

Dedication

This book is dedicated to my wife, Cathlene, who encouraged me to share my insight with others, and to our sons, Cevonn and Maurice, who have embarked on career tracks of their own.

Table of Contents

Figures

Introduction

Throughout the operating life of a large organization there must be a systematic method to categorize, develop, and manage its human resources in order to accomplish the mission. The purpose of this book is to help you understand what this systematic method is, how it works, and how you can adjust and prepare yourself to be more successful in it. The book also provides techniques to help evaluate your status if your progress is not what you think it should be.

There are several forces at work now that are and will continue to impact the level of participation of African-Americans in corporate America.

1. Race is being eliminated as a factor in college admissions and scholarship awards and this may reduce the population of African-Americans entering the workplace.
2. Affirmative action programs throughout the U.S. are being attacked and eliminated.
3. Asian Americans are excelling in colleges and universities and becoming a force in corporate America to be reckoned with.
4. White women have a strong and growing presence in the management ranks.
5. Corporations are flattening their management levels resulting in fewer management positions.

6. The economy is moving from an industrial base to an information (service) base and this is forcing changes in the traditional pyramid organization.
7. The team concept and team decision-making are changing some traditional management concepts.
8. The speed and availability of information is changing the decision making process.

These dynamics and more will require African-Americans to be more prepared with all the necessary skills to progress through and up various organizational structures.

Chapter 1

African-Americans in Corporate America: A Different Perspective

Salaried persons working in a hierarchical organization can be identified as two basic classes. I shall call these the player class and the spectator class. Only the player class can move up in management.

Historically, only two of ten African-Americans who enter the corporate world are considered for meaningful upward mobility, those in the player class. Most discussions about this subject seem to center on the assumption that with the proper tools of competence and skills in gamesmanship, African-Americans, albeit with struggle, can reach the executive offices in larger quantities. This assumption is flawed. As in the White corporate population where only the player class moves, only can the African-American player class move up. The significant difference is about 85 percent of the white population are eligible for the player class while only about 20 percent of the African-American population has this same opportunity. The distinction of these classes is key in effectively discussing this subject because different techniques are required by each class of African-Americans if more overall success is to be gained. I do not believe the distinction of these classes as it relates to African-Americans, and the implications of its importance in attacking the problems, have been heretofore pointed out succinctly.

In my opinion, the corporate world, or any hierarchical organization, considers for meaningful upward mobility only 20 percent or less of those African-Americans who enter. Stated another way, only about two out of ten in any organization are allowed or helped to compete. The rest are not allowed to enter the competition and are relegated to staff and low supervisory roles. Corporations use two basic principles of traditional organizational and management theory, which deny and/or hamper access to middle and upper management positions for African-Americans. These principles are hierarchy of management, and promotions for performance. These are necessary principles but mask the real discrimination and make it appear that African-Americans are not as qualified as the majority.

The hierarchy of management principle requires fewer people to fill management slots as job responsibilities increase at the higher levels. The pyramid finally decreases to an apex at the top. In corporate America, only two of ten African-Americans who enter the pyramid at the bottom are allowed or helped to climb the pyramid. In contrast, I believe eight of ten Whites who enter are allowed or helped to climb the pyramid. Although this pyramid is dynamic and has, and will continue to change as the economy transitions from an industrial base to an information (service) base, it will still be the dominant model in most organizations although other models such as teams will thrive within this pyramid structure.

With the hierarchy of management principle setting the course, the promotion for performance principle maintains the course. Those allowed or helped to compete, the player class - those considered "promotable" get good to excellent performance ratings, which is their ticket to advancement. On the other hand, the spectator class - those considered to have low or no promotability potential, receives average or below performance ratings which hold them in the lower rungs of the organization. This group contains people of all ethnic backgrounds who are not allowed to compete for significant upward mobility based on their true ability or performance. The end results are the same for all individuals - none will make meaningful progress in management.

Therefore, with only about 20 percent of the African-American population who enter an organization allowed or helped to compete, most will peak (reach the glass ceiling) long before getting to the executive levels. There has been much talked and written about the glass ceiling. It is a clear and ever-present phenomenon that is not going away soon. As a matter of fact, if history is any indication, I do not see the results changing much in the next 20 years unless drastic changes are made in the system.

Studies of data collected continue to show that all minorities comprise less than two percent of senior executives, a percentage that has not changed since the late 1970s. In 1996, it came to light that several senior Texaco officials had been recorded making insulting remarks about African-Americans and diversity efforts. The Company's statistics revealed that less than one percent of those earning more than $106,000 were African-Americans and none of the 49 highest paid senior executives were African-Americans.

A higher percentage of African-Americans must get into the player class before greater progress in management can be made. A first step to more progress is to recognize the existence of these two classes of corporate citizens. Afterward, African-Americans need to design and implement separate strategies to help each class within its population. Whites need to change the attitudes that have fueled the system in its disproportionate treatment of us.

I arrived at my ideas after developing during the mid 1970s what I called the "Butler's Philosophy." It states that college degreed salaried workers entering the workforce in a hierarchical organization fall into three categories:

Category 1 (C-1) - Those who will attain middle management positions regardless of perceived performance against peers.
Category 2 (C-2) - Those who will attain middle management positions because of perceived performance against peers.
Category 3 (C-3) - Those who will never achieve middle management positions regardless of outstanding performance against peers.

Earlier in my career or better stated, " my work life," I was fortunate enough to be in a top Fortune 10 company that hired many young engineers. The company had a management-oriented philosophy and each White engineer was considered a potential manager until proven otherwise. This environment gave me an excellent opportunity to view a very successful company's methods, politics and its management selection and development process.

After several years I became very frustrated at my lack of being developed for upward mobility. None of the other African-American engineers were being developed either at that time in this corporate location, however most of the White engineers were in the player class, and many were being groomed and promoted. I felt I had the credentials, background and performance levels needed to be in the main. I had an electrical engineering degree, an MBA from a school in the top 20 ranking at that time, and two years as a commissioned officer in the U. S. Army with combat zone experience in Vietnam. However, my credentials didn't seem to matter at all and the reality of the situation began to become apparent to me after several years. Although the African-American engineers were just as qualified and our performance was as good as most Whites and better than many, we were not being judged by the same criteria as they were. There were some other factors being used besides desire, technical competence and real performance and I was determined to identify those factors.

I looked for an answer to help me explain the stagnation of the African-American engineers. Through close observation of the things taking place, I developed the "Butler's Philosophy" and posted it on my office walls. Visitors, including White supervisors and coworkers, would come by and it soon became a conversation starter for many. In this organization I observed three categories of employees, and the key factors used to manage the future careers of these categories were the performance and potential ratings. I began to look at various individuals and to categorize them as C-1, C-2, or C-3 depending on the training, development and promotions they were being given. Since then, I have observed the phenomenon enough in various other settings and I am convinced it can be generalized to fit most hierarchical organizations; public or private, and military, governmental or industrial.

Entry level personnel in a hierarchical organization can be grouped into the three categories mentioned earlier. I will focus on their attainment of middle management positions because if one does not get to this level he/she will not go higher. The performance and potential ratings are the tools used to facilitate this process and manage the more successful careers of the "promotables" (C-1s & C-2s), and the least successful careers of the "nonpromotables" (C-3s).

Category 1 individuals are those who attain middle management positions primarily because of factors other than excelling in performance against peers. Many of these individuals are bright, intelligent, capable, and ambitious and may perform at the top 25 percent of their peer group (the level needed to compete for middle management and above in most organizations), but they are also in a privileged and distinct class because of other factors. These factors include: having graduated from a certain school; being a part of a well respected or wealthy family; belonging to a certain fraternal, social, religious or political organization; or being related to those in power. Many of these individuals go on to top management positions.

Category 2 individuals do not have the benefits and privileges of those in C-1. However the organization has an open mind. What they do and how they do it can make or break them. They have a good image, are usually conservative, assertive, and show a sense of urgency in things they do. These persons are usually well liked and are good communicators. They earn or receive performance ratings in the top 25 percent of their peer group, which allow them to rise in the organization.

Category 3 persons will never reach middle management levels regardless of how good their performance is in relation to their peers in C-1 or C-2. These are usually the "black sheep" or "mavericks". They have either a poor image via dress or grooming, verbal communications, or are perceived to have unpleasant or obnoxious personality traits. Or maybe these individuals were just born on the "wrong side of the street," i.e. cultural, racial, ethnic, or religious differences from those in power. Keep in mind, no person regardless of color or creed will experience significant upward mobility from within this category. In organizations where promotions are based on a formally managed system of performance, these persons will never get in the top percentiles to allow them to advance.

There is a vast difference in the percentages of Whites and African-Americans in these three categories. My estimates are derived from my observations over 30 years of competing and working in and around military, government and industrial organizations. The population of Whites entering the corporate world fit a normal curve with about 15 percent falling in C-1, about 70 percent falling in C-2 and about 15 percent falling in C-3. Therefore, 85 percent make the player class and are eligible to compete for higher level positions. They can go as high as their circumstances, good fortune, and total skills will allow them.

However, on the other hand, the major portion of the African-American population is invariably placed in C-3. This group is never invited to even try out for the team so they never become players and therefore get no opportunity to be cut or traded along the way. African-Americans estimates per category are; one to two percent in C-1, 15 -18 percent in C-2, and about 80 percent in C-3.

Comparing my estimates, 85 percent of all Whites in the salaried positions entering organizations are eligible to move up the organization, whereas 80 percent of the African-American population is not. Only the 20 percent of the African-American population in C-1 and C-2 are eligible. Stated another way, about eight of ten African-Americans who enter the corporate arena or other hierarchical organizations will only achieve staff and lower level supervisory positions regardless of true performance or potential against peers.

The 20 percent of the African-Americans who are in C-1 and C-2 are competing with the Whites and other groups in those respective categories. It is extremely difficult for those, yet with the right temperament, breaks, guidance, and motivation, most can make some progress, but only a few will make excellent progress.

A higher percentage of the African-Americans entering these organizations will have to get into C-1 and C-2 before any meaningful progress can be achieved. This can only be done through a cooperative effort between the white power structure and the African-American aspirants. The first step in making this happen is acknowledgment by both Whites and African-Americans that such categories exist which has little to do with performance. Secondly, the deleterious affect this poor resource utilization has on the African-Americans and the organizations that employ them must be acknowledged. Lastly, those in power must evaluate and change a system that eliminates eight of ten.

Change may be occurring gradually. I am hearing and reading more and more about those who do acknowledge the reality of this poor resource utilization as opined by Daniel Gross in the publication *Investment News* dated August 2, 1999.

> "Finally they (CEOs of major corporations) realize that the main argument against affirmative action - namely that America is a meritocracy where only performance matters-is only half true. On Wall Street, and in the corporate world, merit is certainly paramount. But relationships can be even more important.....Wall Street veterans do business with classmates from business schools, or with people they started out with on the trading

> floors, or with their Hampton tennis and golf partners. And sadly, Wall Street titans encounter rather few non-whites in these endeavors.....It's a rule of thumb that applies just as much at Joe's Diner as it does at Chase Manhattan Bank: people hire people they know. Wall Street is filled with the children of well connected movers and shakers who owe their jobs more to parents' contacts than to their class ranking."

The last sentence of the quote is a prime example of those I defined as being in C-1.

Furthermore, African-Americans need to be much more proactive by targeting the self-help efforts to the various categories. One size does not fit all. Strategies and tactics for the C-1s and C-2s must be handled as a coach would train and prepare those already on the team who compete in the games. The latter category, which comprises most African-Americans who are the spectators on the sidelines, would benefit most from strategies and tactics that provide skills and techniques to help them make the team. Remember, the key to more success for African-Americans is to develop characteristics that allow us to be identified as a C-1 or C-2. For once an individual is pegged as a C-3, his or her career is usually forever capped at low level jobs within that organization.

Several years after developing my theory, I saw an article by Robert Jackall in the Harvard Business Review, September-October, 1983, entitled " Moral Maze: Bureaucracy and Managerial Work". Here are a few excerpts.

"It is within this complicated and ambiguous authority structure, always subject to upheaval, that success and failure are meted out to those in the middle and upper middle management ranks. Managers rarely spoke to me of objective criteria for achieving success because once certain crucial points in one's career are passed, success or failure seems to have little to do with one's accomplishments. Rather, success is socially defined and distributed. Corporations do demand, of course, a basic competence and sometimes specified training and experience; (but) hiring practices usually insures these. A weeding-out process takes place, however, among the lower ranks of managers during the first several years of their experience. By the time a manager reaches a certain numbered grade in the ordered hierarchy,.....managerial competence as such is taken for granted and assumed not to differ greatly from one manager to the next. The focus then switches to social factors, which are determined by authority and political alignments - the fealty structure - and by the ethos and style of the corporation.

Surely, one might argue, there must be more to success in the corporation than style, personality, team play, chameleonic adaptability, and fortunate connections. What about the bottom line - profits, performance?

Unquestionably, 'hitting the numbers' - that is, meeting the profit commitments already discussed is important, but only within the social context I have described. There are

> several rules here. First, no one in a line position - that is with profit and loss responsibility who regularly 'misses his numbers' will survive, let alone rise. Second, a person who always hits his numbers but who lacks some or all of the required social skills will not rise. Third, a person who sometimes misses his numbers but who has all the desirable social traits will rise.
>
> Performance is thus always subject to a myriad of interpretations. Profits matter, but it is much more important in the long run to be perceived as 'promotable' by belonging to central political networks. Patrons protect those selected as rising stars from the negative judgments of others; and only the foolhardy point out even egregious errors of those in power or those destined for it."

More recently, Glen C. Loury, professor of economics at Boston University and author, in an editorial in late 1996 about the Texaco case, which I referred to earlier, had this to say. "...Outsiders or lower-level employees are seldom privy to the complex deliberations and raft of subjective judgments that go into the selection of the top people in any large, complex organization."

Chapter 2

The Process of Determining Upward Mobility

The level of upward mobility achieved in an organization usually results from the following two processes in human resource (HR) management: (1) Assessment of an individual's performance in a current job, called the performance rating or evaluation; and, (2) An estimate of the person's potential to achieve higher levels of responsibility in the organization, called the potential or promotability rating or evaluation. This process for most African-American aspirants, instead of being a beneficial one, ends up becoming what I call the "performance trap". Once the performance trap has engulfed an individual, there is little he/she can do to achieve middle or upper management positions within that organization. Three choices are available; plight, fight, or flight. Sadly, all invoke some penalty on the African-American employees. He can stay and accept this plight, stay and fight the system through various means, or book a flight to another organization where he can get a new start.

Many organizations and the powerful people who control them never admit the existence of a class structure as I have succinctly defined. Regardless of whether it is formerly defined or acknowledged (which I doubt), or implied through the organization's culture, it is real, alive and functioning. But the tools used to mask and maintain this class structure, and deny meaningful access to higher levels of management for African-Americans (or any person), are the performance and promotability (potential) rating systems. In the class structure, a C-3 will never progress beyond staff or low supervisory positions regardless of real performance or potential because they will receive average or below marks in these critical assessment areas.

The first of the two HR management tools is the performance rating. Two key questions arise regarding performance. First, what is it? In this context, it is an attempted measurement of the key variables determined to be important to the success of an individual when evaluated against the requirements of a specific job. These measurements can be objective or subjective.

Secondly, how is performance measured? There are four common approaches in use as follows: (1) the performance by objectives (results-oriented); (2) the peer group performance (comparison-based); (3) the skills/character method (performer-based) and (4) the personality/style (behavior based). Some organizations use a combination of the above and there are advantages and disadvantages to each.

In the results-oriented approach, simply put, the individual and his immediate supervisor develop a set of objectives to be accomplished over a period of time with performance based on the timing of completion, complexity, quality and volumes of work produced. The advantages to this method are that it is tailored to the priorities of the job; employees know how performance will be measured and; it facilitates communication between superior and subordinate. Disadvantages include the facts that it is task-oriented, time-consuming and hard to administer.

In the comparison-based approach, simply stated, the individual is evaluated by one or more supervisory/management personnel against others who are in similar jobs at similar grade levels and skills. It is based on the simple fact that almost everything in the universe follows a normal distribution. Advantages are its intuitive merit and the fact that it can be easily understood. A big disadvantage of this method is its high subjectivity and potential for abuse or misuse. Other influence factors that can and do cloud the evaluation include the quality of the supervisor/subordinate relationship, friendships, alliances, associations, alumni affiliation, religion, national origin, ethnic background, and of course, race. The types of organizations where the Butler's Philosophy is more evident are the ones that use the comparison-based and the performer-based types of performance evaluation.

The performer-based system uses skills and character traits to rate the individual. Advantages are uniformity of factors, easy identification of the factors and ease of administration. Disadvantages are the factors may not be job specific, they may not measure results, there are no job standards per se, and it may tend not to depict true performance.

The behavior-based approach attempts to identify behaviors that are important in the job success. Advantages are predicated in the assumption that its use is based on a detailed job analysis and therefore behaviors are job-specific. The key disadvantages are its construction is lengthy and complex, it does not focus on results and does not lend itself well to the job evaluation of managers and executives.

In recent years, there has been a greater emphasis on a performance appraisal approach called the "360". It also may be called other related names. In this approach the organization requires the immediate rater formally to seek performance feedback from those who work closest surrounding the rated person, i.e., his/her immediate superior, subordinates, peers, and customers/clients, hence the name "360".

Performance evaluation systems are necessary in human resource development and management so I am in concurrence with the use of such methods. I believe the results-oriented approach is the best of the methods because it is less subjective. It focuses on the mission, goals and objectives, and compares accomplishments against the job requirements. The "360" approach adds a positive element to all of the others since it tends to average out biases of any sort. I've always advocated that peers doing the same or similar jobs can often provide better insight than management about who among them is doing the best job. In the main, however, the use of a performer-based evaluation system of any sort is detrimental to most African-Americans because we are often perceived beforehand not to be as capable as the majority.

The second of the two primary HR management tools is the potential or promotability rating. This rating determines how high one is expected to go in the organization and is usually kept a lot more secretive than the performance rating. Working within the hierarchial grade level or rank level system the evaluator(s) rate the person by one of the following methods:

1. Person is expected to go one or more levels above his/her current level.
2. Person is expected to reach a certain graded level within the hierarchy.
3. Person is expected to reach lower (staff), middle, or upper management levels.

This potential rating is based on perceived or rated performance along with several other factors described below and discussed further in Chapter 3:

1. The type of image the rated person projects.
2. The level of distinction the rated person has.
3. The rated person's perceived ability to "fit" within the "culture".
4. The current management's comfort level with the rated person.

It is important to note that there is a strong positive correlation between the performance and potential ratings of C-1 and C-2 persons as the forthcoming Figures 1 and 2 depict. In other words, a higher performance rating usually results in a higher potential rating and visa versa. However, there are many cases where a high performance in a current job will not result in a high potential rating. A classic example is the rating of a C-3 person but there are others. Chapter 5 will provide more insight.

Although the foregoing HR management tools are being used very effectively now to deny meaningful upward mobility to most African-Americans, there has always been a reason to justify our exclusion from the main. The argument against our inclusion shifted about thirty years ago from preparation to performance.

Until the late 1960s, African-Americans were denied entry into corporate America because of discrimination, however the main argument was we lacked adequate preparation through education. The civil rights movement created an entree for us and as the doors became ajar, we began to expand our learning and our college majors and degrees beyond the traditional educational fields.

Over the last 30 years we have continued to prepare and improve our knowledge and skills and have made significant progress into the lower levels, however our participation in the middle and especially the upper ranks is uncharacteristically low because we have been systematically denied meaningful access on the grounds that our performance is not competitive with those being promoted.

The performance and potential ratings are the tools, the mechanics, by which African-Americans are included or excluded from upward mobility. I believe pictures will help you to understand these concepts. Let's look at two models shown as Figures 1 and 2 used by those in authority to manage the human resource needs of the organization. Understanding of these models will be very beneficial to your understanding of career management. The first model, Figure 1 is a matrix with four quadrants that shows the importance of the job to the organization on the Y-axis in relation to the individual's performance or expected performance in the job on the X-axis. This model represents jobs at all levels of the organization; entry, lower, middle and upper; and reflects the fact that those in authority are likely to operate the organization with a direct or implied importance to jobs at all levels, and assign individuals to these jobs with this importance in consideration. The higher on the Y-axis and the more to the right on the X-axis, the greater the importance and performance respectively. The matrix reveals the following information:

1. Quadrant 1 (Q-1): Jobs of lower importance and/or visibility. Normally assigned to persons with assumed or rated lower performance.
2. Quadrant 2 (Q-2): Jobs of higher importance usually occupied by persons with assumed or rated lower performance.
3. Quadrant 3 (Q-3): Jobs of higher importance usually occupied by persons with assumed or rated higher performance.
4. Quadrant 4 (Q-4): Jobs of lower importance usually occupied by persons with assumed or rated higher performance.

Figure 1

Typical Importance of Job Versus Individual Performance Matrix

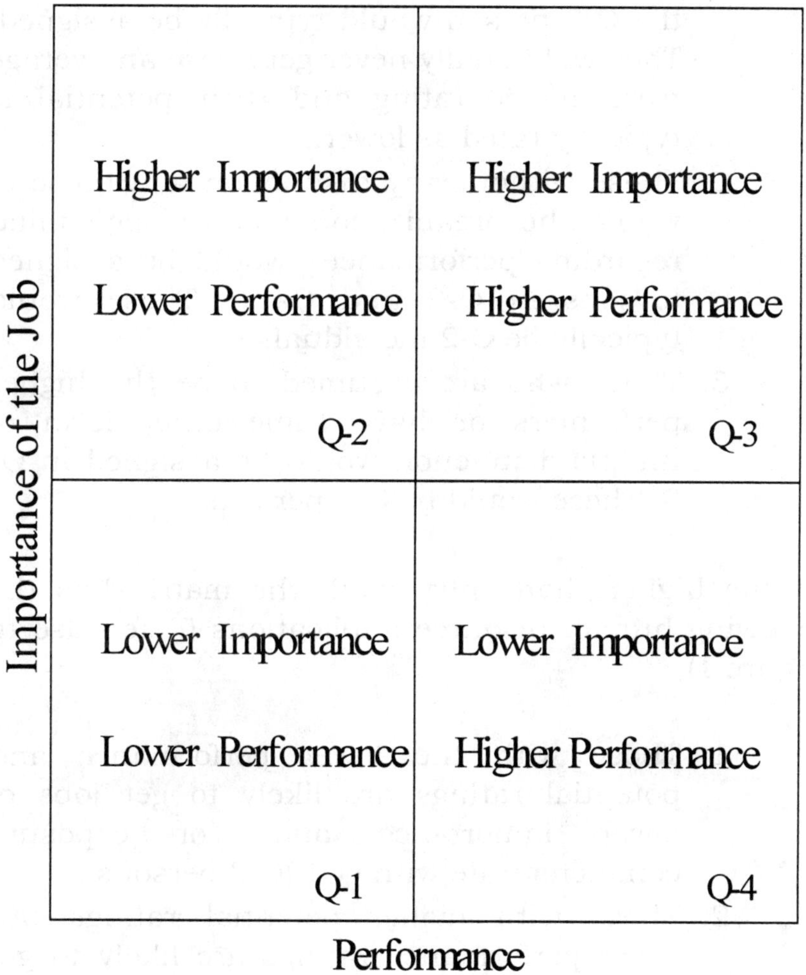

The matrix has the following human resource implications at entry level:

1. Those who are assumed to be the lower performers would be assigned to the jobs with the lower importance and /or visibility which is Q-1 on the matrix. This is where the C-3 person would typically be assigned. They will usually never get above an average performance rating and their potential is typically rated as lower.
2. Those without any distinction and those of whom the organization has an open mind regarding performance would be assigned to jobs in Q-2 and Q-4. These would typically be C-2 individuals.
3. Those who are assumed to be the higher performers or have some other form of unique distinction would be assigned in Q-3. These would be C-1 persons.

At the higher than entry level, the matrix has the following human resource implications (Refer also to Figure 1):

1. Those with the lower performance and potential ratings are likely to get jobs of lower importance and /or exposure commensurate with Q-1 (C-3 persons).
2. Those with higher potential ratings but lower performance ratings are likely to get jobs denoting higher importance and /or exposure in Q-2, C-1 and C-2 persons.

3. Those with the higher performance and potential ratings are likely to get jobs denoting higher importance and /or exposure in Q-3 , C-1 and C-2 persons.
4. Those with higher performance ratings but lower potential ratings are likely to get jobs denoting lower importance and / or exposure in Q-4, C-3 and marginal C-2 persons.

The next model we will examine is shown in Figure 2, which is a matrix that plots potential on the Y-axis and performance on the X-axis for employees at all levels within an organization. The matrix has the following human resource implications at entry level:

1. A person who is assumed to be of lower potential is more likely to get a lower performance rating and visa versa. This is Q-1 where most African-Americans are as C-3s.
2. A person who is assumed to be of higher potential is more likely to get a higher performance rating.

The matrix has the following human resource implications for other than entry levels:

1. A lower rated performance individual (average or below) is likely to be kept at this performance rating and be assigned a lower potential rating consistent with Q-1. These persons will remain in staff and low supervisory positions described for C-3.

Figure 2

Typical Performance Versus Potential Matrix

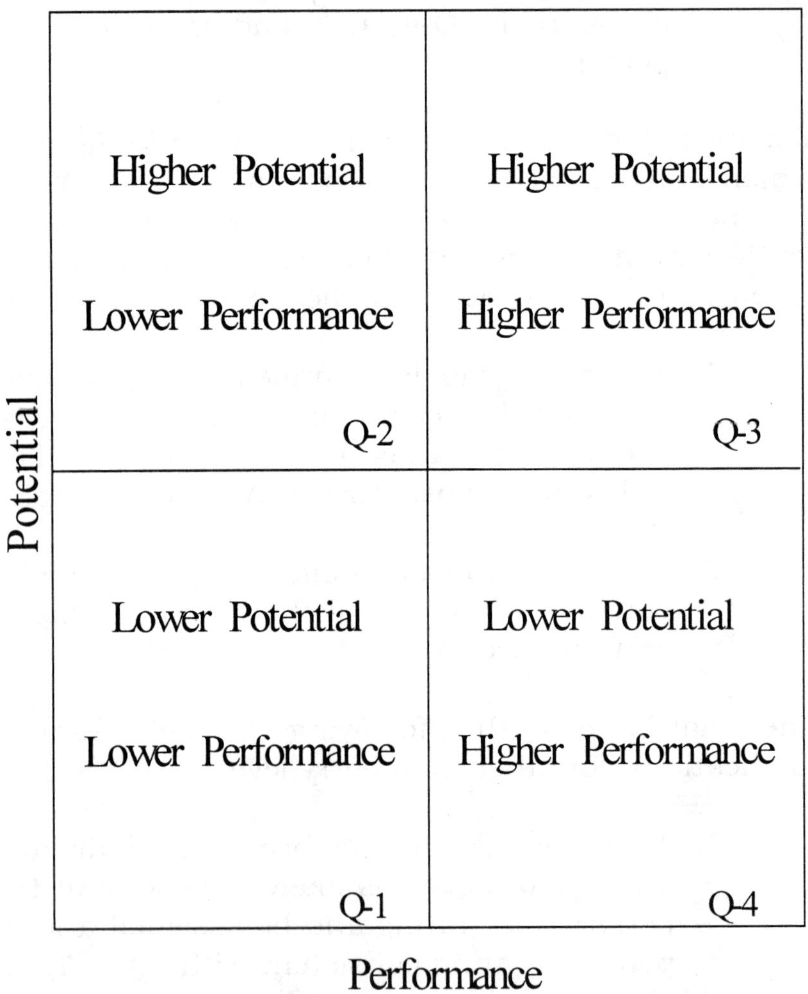

2. Persons in Q-2 include the following: those who have made some career advances but have risen to a level that has exceeded their skills; those who have fallen out of favor with higher management for various reasons; and those who have suffered mental, emotional or physical events that distracted them causing their career progress to stall or stop. These persons come from C-2 (including African-Americans who have reached their glass ceiling).
3. Q-3 people are those who continue to receive favorable treatment and are judged to perform at a level that meets and exceeds expectations. These come from C-1 and C-2 and achieve positions at the highest levels of the organization.
4. The lower potential, higher performer typical of Q-4 is someone who excels in his job and has little aspirations for management, or has been labeled as maverick or eccentric, or does not have adequate people (social) skills. These persons will usually advance up the technical ladder or be perennial supervisors.
5. A person with a Q-2 rating is likely to get more training, coaching, counseling and attention from upper management than a person with a Q-4 rating. In other words, the organization values more highly the person with the higher potential.

So far I have discussed the following topics:

- The premises of the Butler's Philosophy which I believe identifies the real workings of the system
- The fallacy of the backbone criteria of preparation and performance as applied to African-Americans
- The impact of the system on African-Americans
- The principles used to manage career advancement in a hierarchical organization
- Two models (Figures 1 & 2) for human resource management.

To further benefit from this insight one must accept the following statements as key operating assumptions of the hierarchical organization:

1. African-Americans are generally assumed to be lower performers with lower potential than the majority.
2. Jobs in the organization have varying degrees of importance and exposure potential.

Therefore, if we accept these statements as facts (and truths), then, in an entry level position, the first five years are critical to any person's career, and especially so for the African-American. So, it is vitally important for us to avoid the C-3 category because those who are assigned there will usually never progress beyond staff and low supervisory levels because this is the cap for the category. Their assigned performance and potential ratings are average or below, although for many, their true performance and potential are much higher.

An obvious question by now should be, How do most African-Americans get set up for this failure? I'm glad you asked. It happens like this. The above two organizational assumptions operate in tandem, causing corresponding actions by decision-makers beginning at the entry level. Some initial assumption is made about the individual's expected performance and potential based on a perception that was either preconceived by the decision maker(s), or created by the African-American aspirant, either actively or passively.

For example, regarding the first possibility, it is a known fact that colleges and universities are rated, and graduates from the higher rated institutions are expected to be more successful in whatever endeavor they pursue. For those who attended the so called "lower tier" colleges and universities, this perception more often than not creates a lesser expectation of accomplishment and the individual is more than likely to be assigned to a job of lesser overall importance and/or lesser exposure within the hiring organization. This tendency creates a significant hurdle for the new hire since the lower commensurate performance and potential ratings usually follow, often with little change over time, resulting in a corresponding level of stagnation.

I believe there are two key factors that contribute to this problem, inadequate African-American preparation, and racism. First, but not foremost, is inadequate African-American preparation - not inadequate preparation in technical competence but inadequate preparation in "process" competence. Too many African-Americans enter the corporate world with little knowledge of how the

Figure 3

Management Hierarchy

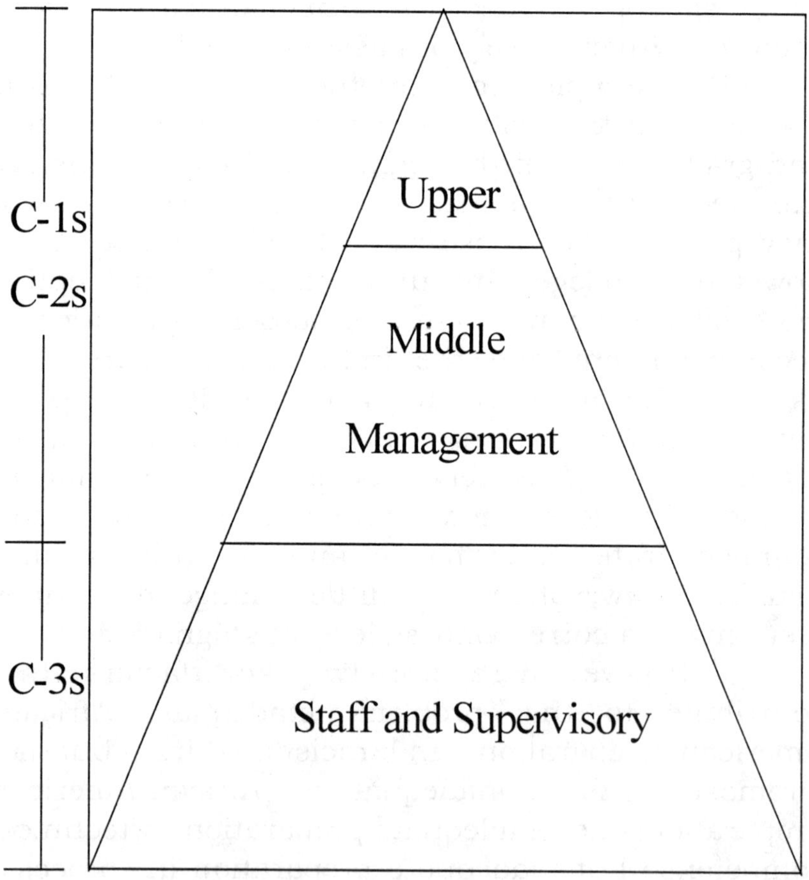

system operates. With little knowledge of the process and little or no mentoring, our lack of process knowledge and our weaknesses play well into the hands of those who have negative perceptions, or we may unknowingly create negative perceptions. By the time we learn the system, it is usually too late to make significant upward mobility within that particular organization because performance and career potential have been rated below the levels needed to reach middle management positions. In other words, we have not been identified as a C-1 or C-2.

Unfortunately, our learning period corresponds with the period in corporate America during which personnel are identified for higher management positions. Most organizations that use some formal method of identifying and developing talent for greater responsibility do this within the first five years of the person's employment. Those who are selected peak further out at various higher levels in their careers but those not selected remain at or near the bottom throughout. Remember, a person will achieve only the levels permitted for the various categories of C-1, C-2, and C-3. So, there is little margin for error on our part and the system is very unforgiving of us.

Figure 3 is a model of the various categories I have defined compared with the three different general levels of management within an organization. C-3 individuals are restricted to the lower levels of the management hierarchy. Middle and upper management are chosen from the C-1 and C-2 .

What length of time does the aspirant have to distinguish him/herself? Figure 4 entitled "Your

Figure 4

Your Window of Opportunity

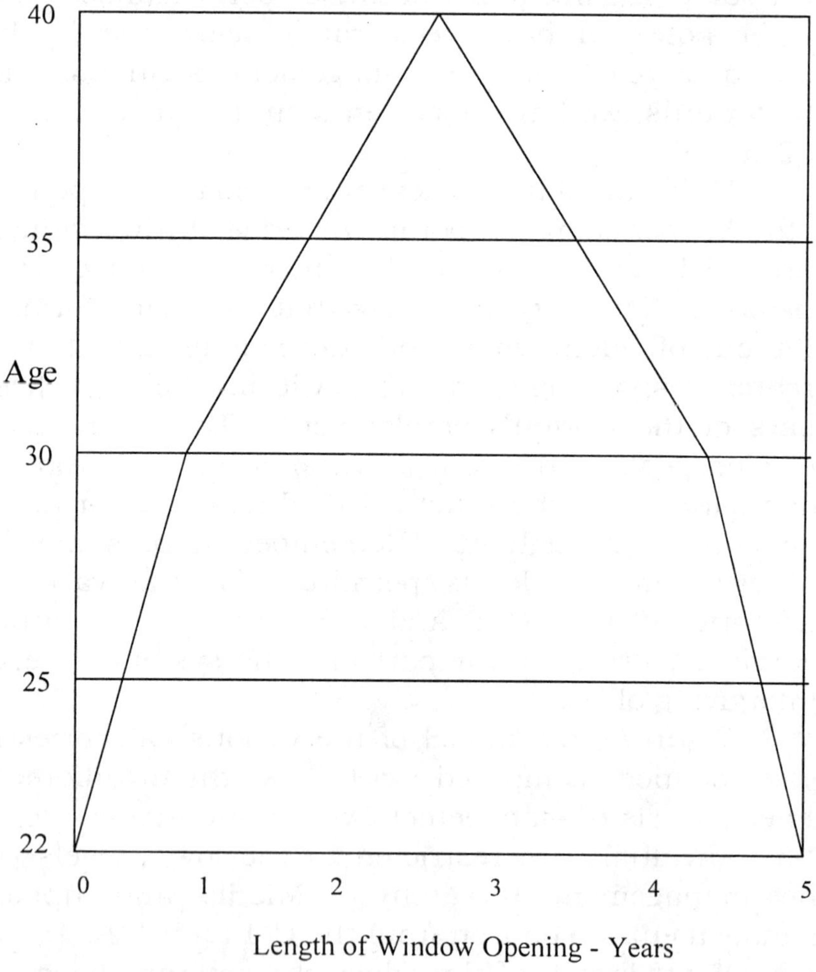

Window of Opportunity" is an estimate of the opening of time in years an individual has to distinguish him or herself as a C-1 or C-2 at the start of the career. Remember, the underlying assumption of this book is that the organization is sizable and has a formal system of career development and progression, and an integrated "pay for performance" system.

The window opening does vary with age and experience. A person who starts a career in such an organization at less than 30 years of age has about five years before the window closes. If a person moves to another organization between the ages of 30-35 years of age, this feat must be accomplished in about three years. The person over 35 years of age and still at a grade and/or pay below that considered middle management has 1 1/2 to 2 years of opening. In a change after 40 years of age, a person who is still in the lower levels of the management ranks will seldom progress more than one, or at best, two grades higher in the new organization. Of course, there are always exceptions to any rule and several exceptions are:

1. The ability to negotiate a special deal.
2. Having a high demand key skill.
3. A special circumstance, i.e., merger, reorganization, or other departure of key people which left a void.
4. Perform a noteworthy or outstanding feat (distinction) that cannot be ignored.
5. Get on the coat tails of a person who is upward bound and he/she decides to take you with them.

6. Be or become politically or socially connected with key decision-makers.

Just as important as the "open window" period criteria, and in parallel with it, is the performance criterion. One who aspires to middle management and above must obtain his/her first performance rating above the threshold set by the organization, or reach it by the second review, and maintain this performance rating. This threshold is a performance rating usually above the 75th percentile - in top 25%.

Inadequate African-American preparation is a continuing challenge, however as previously stated, it is usually not from a lack of technical competence, but it stems from the general weakness in our ability to build consensus and influence others. In the main however, our deficiencies in preparation are less than half the challenge. What prevents the person from making substantial upward mobility who possesses the important career influence factors (CIFs) I will describe in the next chapter? This person could have had those characteristics when he/she entered the organization or they could have been acquired along the way.

There are two main reasons. Racism and bureaucracy have placed the individual in C-3. There is a floor level of performance needed to remain employed but top level performance does not insure progress for most African-Americans. The old adage that "cream rises to the top" does not work well or often in our case. Only a very few real superstars make significant progress in this system.

The second and more profound reason African-Americans don't rise is discrimination caused by racism. Proponents for eliminating affirmative action will indicate they are color blind when it comes to job performance evaluation and other selection decisions. Anyone who tells me this causes my alarms to be triggered. America is a color conscious society, however the more money and power a person of color has, the less likely the manifestation of the effects.

Two key assumptions are made that form the difference in treatment of African-Americans and the majority. First, racism starts by assuming that most African-Americans cannot perform at levels commensurate to Whites and we must prove otherwise. Therefore, almost all African-Americans start and continue through their careers proving they can do a competitive job. We are scrutinized more closely, held in jobs longer, and the system is less forgiving of our mistakes and shortcomings. This alone requires African-Americans to be better than many Whites they are in competition with.

Conversely, Whites are assumed to be capable from the start and they must prove themselves otherwise. They are given a chance, trained and given responsibility, and many of the average or below are "carried", while more qualified African-Americans are held back and contemplated about. This kind of system allows only the exceptional African-Americans to rise while most of the above average become stagnated in C-3 and the truly average African-Americans are asked to resign or are fired. Yet those who manage these systems will tell you there are few or no "qualified" African-Americans to be found that can perform at competitive levels.

Once the system has placed a bonafide African-American C-1 or C-2 in the C-3 category, bureaucracy keeps him/her there. The sad fact is once a person is placed in C-3, he will usually never get out as long as he is in that organization. There is little or no transition between the categories.

To illustrate, the concept is similar to dealing with bureaucracies such as public school systems and the various levels of government. A word was introduced into our vocabulary over the last 10-15 years in relation to the public school system called "tracking." Children are put on a fast, slow or special track early in their school lives and usually remain on that track throughout their school lives. This track determines the kind and quality of training and development they get in preparing them to make a meaningful contribution to society later in life. Those (most African-American males in the public school systems) on the slow or special tracks are at a grave disadvantage. For example, a child is given a label in the early school years such as a "special ed" or "special needs" child. This student is put on a "track" and could remain there over an extended period unless the parents or some school official recognizes differently and challenges the system to review and change the evaluation if warranted. The child may have only needed some eyeglasses to correct a vision deficiency.

The fact that tracking occurs in public school systems and the fact that it places many African-American students at a big disadvantage should not be a surprise. A recent study, along with others over the last few years, documents this fact. A series of studies initiated by The Civil Rights Project at Harvard University and released on March 2, 2001 indicated that African-American students are 2.9 times as likely as Whites to be identified as mentally retarded. Researchers said one of their most troubling findings was that African-American boys living in wealthier communities with better schools and more White classmates were at a greater risk of being labeled "mentally retarded" than those in predominantly African-American, low income schools. The lead sentence of the article about the study in the Forth Worth Star-Telegram daily newspaper began this way. "Texas and Forth Worth data parallel national studies that say Black students end up in special education classes in disproportionate numbers, setting them apart for life and saddling them with less demanding work and lower expectations." My points exactly.

Another example is city hall. If taxing authorities erroneously assesses taxes, the impacted property owner usually has to go through an inordinate amount of paperwork and red tape, at different departments and levels, to correct the situation.

If the above systems were not challenged, such errors would probably never get corrected, or at least they would not get corrected in a timely manner. Likewise, in corporations, tracking (the performance and potential rating systems) occurs which determines the kind and quality of training and development one gets in preparing them for greater upward mobility. Very few managers are willing to champion the cause of one (regardless of race or ethnicity) who has been labeled erroneously. It takes too much time and effort and in addition, organizational cultures discourage this effort. Besides to do this, albeit the right thing, would defeat the purpose of having a C-3 category which is the soldier base of the organization.

In conclusion, racism has a more deleterious effect on African-American progress than inadequate preparation. And institutional and systemic racism are well entrenched in corporate America as recent cases at a Wall Street firm, Texaco, Coca Cola, and Microsoft have proven. A perception exists that most African-Americans are sub par performers, i.e. the performance trap, and results in a low percentage of African-Americans in the competition classes of C-1 and C-2. The truth of the matter is that many African-Americans in C-3 can and are performing at levels commensurate with persons in C-1 and C-2 but have been handicapped by their ratings. This negative perception could be changed if we were looked at as individuals rather than as a group and the problem could be corrected almost immediately if organizations were truly color blind and used the same criteria for all participants.

Many more of us, regardless of the communities we grew up in, or the schools we attended, have the ability and capability to be much more successful in the hierarchical organization. Affirmative action attempted to give us more of an equal opportunity but with the dismantling of these efforts in many circles beginning in the college admissions, current gains may be seriously hampered.

Chapter 3

Developing Your Career Influence Factors

Given these hurdles, how can young African-American graduates overcome them? First they must be aware of the system rules. Secondly, they must have characteristics synonymous with C-1 and C-2 individuals. Most things happen in this world as a result of some event or person being able to exert influence either positively or negatively. The few African-Americans in C-1 and C-2 have been able to influence to their advantage (positively); those in C-3 influenced to their disadvantage (negatively).

Success in this environment usually requires a proactive approach. Although you will find some African-Americans that have prospered in the system who initially got their start passively, i.e., they were unaware of the process dynamics but luck and fate carried them, this is by far the exception rather than the rule.

Many African-Americans enter the corporate world thinking that technical competence in their respective discipline and hard work will be their ticket to upward mobility. After all, this is the "American Way." Many others after years of frugal living just want to get a good job and earn some "money". Actions based solely on either idea are

Figure 5

A Dual Stairway is Required For Success

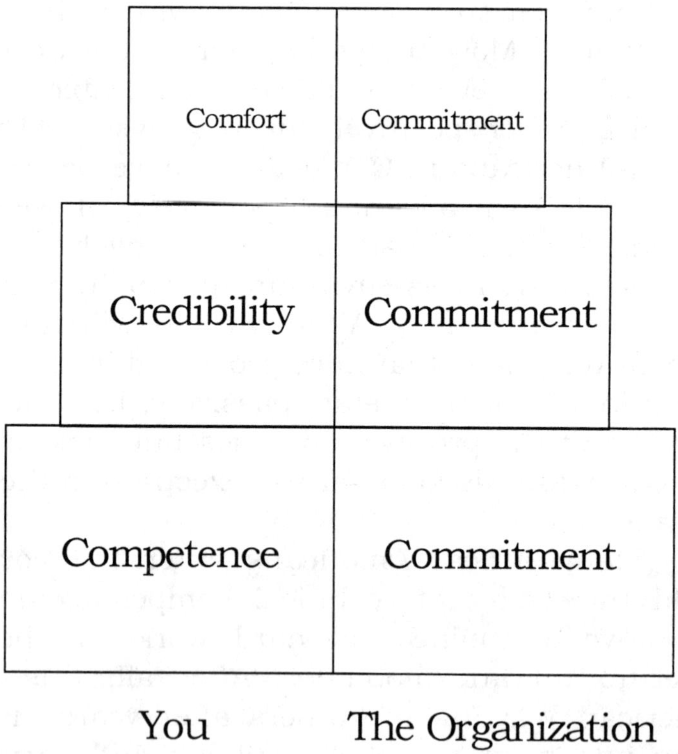

likely to have the same results unless changed, or they get lucky; C-3 with a career in lower supervisory or technical staff positions with average or below performance ratings.

A dual stairway must be used to insure more success of the African-American professional as modeled in the base form in Figure 5. The employee must climb three stairs in order to be considered for the meaningful upward progress and these three stairs are comprised of the following characteristics; COMPETENCE, CREDIBILITY and COMFORT. Competence is having the technical skills to do the job you were hired for and the ability to communicate with others whom you must interface. Credibility is having the character and integrity that reflect soundness, honesty, and reliability. Lastly, you must be comfortable with yourself that you have a right to be there and act with the self-assurance so the organization is convinced you should be there.

The organization must climb three steps with you; COMMITMENT, COMMITMENT and COMMITMENT. First, the organization must be committed to insure you an opportunity to compete fairly with the technical skills you have. Secondly, the organization must be committed to insure you have the opportunity to exercise your character and integrity to the highest extent possible in carrying out your assigned responsibilities. Thirdly, the organization must be committed to providing you an environment that is comfortable enough for you to prove to them you have a right to be there. This environment should be free of racism, sexism and discrimination of all sorts. It should have adequate workplace amenities; clear policies, procedures and expectations; and clear criteria for determining performance.

The basic stairway alone, however, is not enough and will seldom carry a person above the levels permitted for a C-3. Having said the above, there are certain things that must be put in the proper perspective. So far I have not said anything about strong academic performance and very little about technical competence and good moral character. I personally believe very strongly a person should strive to achieve excellence in these areas as well as in every other positive aspect of his life, especially now since knowledge is exploding and the world is faced with more difficult and complex moral issues.

However, my observation in most of corporate America is that technical competence in one's discipline and good moral character alone are only sufficient enough to get and keep a job but are not the most critical for upward advancement. A person with only those strengths in the highly competitive organization is a most likely candidate for C-3. While high academic performance will usually get you in the door first and strong character is respected, I believe there are more important factors for management progression. As a matter of fact, most African-Americans have the technical competence to be successful in the majority of jobs in corporate America. My jobs as an engineer in the manufacturing sector have demanded only a small percentage of the math and science learned in the attainment of an electrical engineering degree.

I have identified six critical factors important for success in the corporate world and I shall call them Career Influence Factors (CIFs). Your CIFs are the anchor to your stairway to success and are shown in Figure 6. Of course, these CIFs that follow presume a person has an intense desire to be successful:

1. Technical skills
2. Communications skills
3. Personality and social skills
4. Admirable uniqueness (Distinction)
5. Intensity (Energy)
6. Sense of urgency

Technical skills and technical competence are different by my definition with the latter being only one component of the former so let me first distinguish between the two. I refer to technical competence as knowledge in one's major or discipline of study; however, technical skills involve more than knowledge in one's discipline. It also involves overall know how, that is, knowing how to get things done, i.e., to get good results by using a combination of training, and other gifted or acquired talents and abilities. It is not only knowing the answer to a technical question but also knowing where to look for a solution to a problem or challenge and how to

Figure 6

Your Career Influence Factors (CIFs)
Anchor to Your Stairway to Success

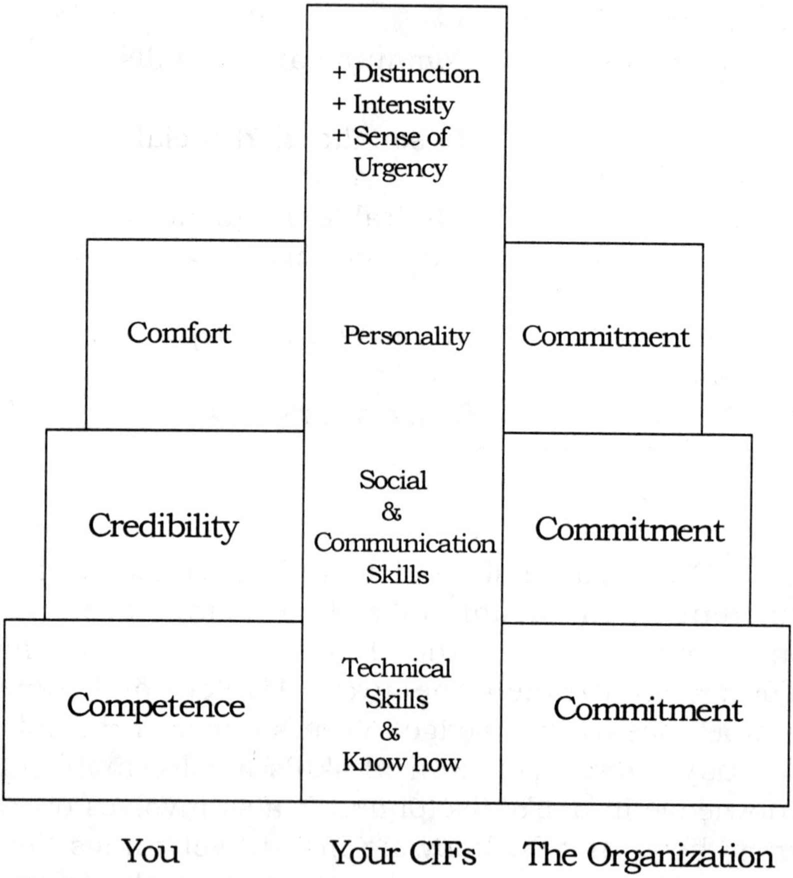

synthesize information from a variety of sources into a coherent and useful application.

The ability to communicate both orally and written is the next important CIF. A person who knows the facts and circumstances and can articulate them to others in a clear, concise and logical manner builds self-confidence and establishes credibility. The following statistics should magnify the value of good business communications:

- Success in business is over 80 percent dependent on effective communication and interpersonal skills.
- Seventy (70) percent of workforce mistakes are attributable to poor communications.
- Fifty-five (55) percent of a person's message is communicated nonverbal.
- The average worker spends 50 percent of his/her time communicating.
- The average worker spends 45 percent of his/her communicating time listening.
- The average worker spends nine percent of his/her communicating time writing.

Therefore, a person who has a little less technical competence but who communicates well is usually more in demand for management than the opposite.

Figure 7 describes this point well. It shows the types of skills needed at the various levels of management. Jobs at entry level require a contribution of about 50 percent from one's technical skills, which has already been discussed, and about 50 percent from one's consensus-building skills in order for the employee to be successful.

Figure 7

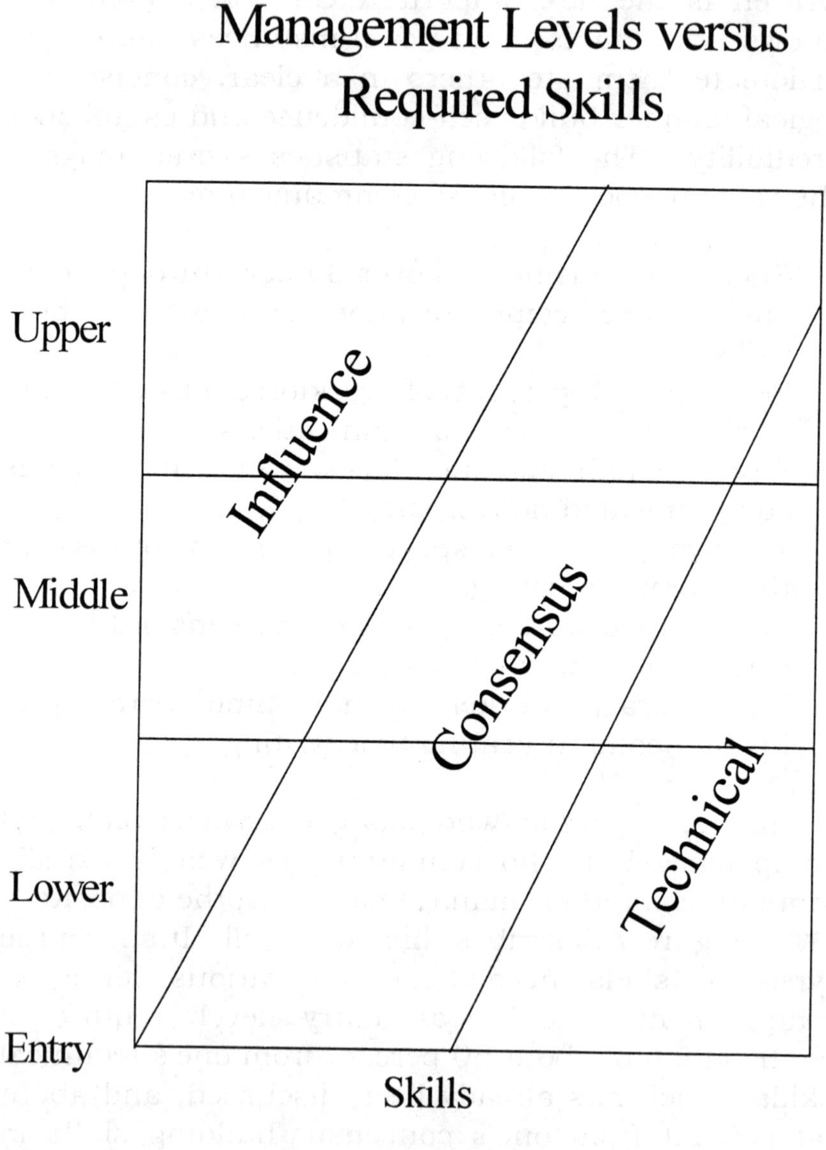

Management Levels versus
Required Skills
Upper
Middle
Lower
Entry
Influence
Consensus
Technical
Skills

Consensus skills include communications (both written and spoken), interpersonal relations, and persuasion. All involve the use of your personality and character traits in getting people to agree or go along with your point of view - that is, the ability positively to influence people in a team environment. Since one has little or no power or authority at the entry levels, their accomplishments must be made and recognized through the technical and consensus arenas. As one moves up the management hierarchy the value and the need for the three types of skills change; technical skills decrease in value and need while consensus and influence skills become more valuable.

The middle management levels require a balanced combination of all three skills. At the lowest levels of middle management one needs to have a proportionate mix of all. About 1/3 of the skills needed to be successful will come from the technical area, about 1/3 from the consensus area, and about 1/3 from the influence area.

At the upper management levels the influence skills reign supreme, ranging from 50 percent to 75 percent of the total job requirements, while the consensus skills needed range between 25 percent to 40 percent, and technical skills required are on the order of magnitude of 10 percent or less.

Let's take a closer look at this concept called influence. As stated earlier, all of us have the ability and do exert influence on those people with whom we come in contact or interface. Influence is gained from three areas: (1) the power of organizational authority; (2) the personal power of distinction; and (3) the personal power of persuasion. Persuasion can be defined as the ability to clarify a vision or message within oneself and so articulate it to others that they believe in, receive it as their own, and follow leadership willingly in pursuit of it.

William Oncken in *Managing Management Time* states, "Managerial influence derives not only from your competence, but from others confidence in your competence.... not from your personality, but from others' rapport with your personality.... and not from your character, but from respect for your character."

We should now return a look at Figure 6 to discuss the remaining CIFs. Personality is the third CIF that plays an important role in success. Personality is the window through which others see us. Are we friendly, helpful, talkative, moody, etc? An excellent personality combined with acceptable technical skills and strong communications skills increases one's probability of succeeding in management. A person who is well liked by most is often seen as someone who can work through others to get things done. In other words, he/she is often viewed as a potential manager.

As stated by Robert Jackall in his article referenced earlier, "Managers emphasized the importance of 'being fast on your feet'... and possessing a subtle, almost indefinable sophistication, marked especially by an urbane, witty, graceful, engaging, and friendly demeanor."

Libraries are replete with information about personality types, and numerous tests are available to identify types and styles in various interpersonal relationship settings. The Myers/Briggs assessment is probably one of the most widely known of these types of tools. There have been numerous studies done on what personality and character traits help make a successful career. A greater understanding of personality types, how you relate to other types, and how others may relate to your type can lead to greater harmony, communications, and productivity. Therefore, my advice is to learn as much as you can about yourself and others through these personality assessment tools. Many organizations provide such assessments in their hiring and also in their staff development training programs.

To review, I have identified six CIFs, and I believe the latter three, when combined with the former three, make the winning formula. These are; an admirable uniqueness or distinction, intensity, and a sense of urgency. These help to set the individual apart from others who possess the first three CIFs.

The first in this latter grouping is distinction (admirable uniqueness). This distinction would include but is not limited to a particular skill, ability, accomplished feat, strong personality, strong character or a combination of these. It has to be something that is innate and uniquely sets one person apart from another, something that separates him/her from the crowd or competition. For example, one may have naturally developed a strong presence, either through physical stature or effective communications. A particular "station in life" (family name, school) is a source of distinction for many.

The second and third CIFs in this latter grouping, intensity and sense of urgency, will often distinguish the person from the rest of the crowd, particularly when combined with distinction. Intensity is that burning drive to accomplish a task or goal. It is the force which makes a person - when all is said and done - take one more lap, go one more round, make one more call, read one more report, before quitting for the day.

Sense of urgency is the demeanor and character in a person that helps focus on priority items and act according to the old adage which says, "Never put off for tomorrow what you can do today." These three traits are admired greatly and the person who displays them has a very positive influence on decision-makers in the organization.

Speaking of the ability to influence positively, it may be helpful to see what some experts say on the subject. According to several studies, truly successful people are those who know how to cooperate with others, eschew combat, and demonstrate a talent for compromise.

"High achievers are healthier than the norm, have better than average relationships, and are successful in both work and love", according to Charles A. Garfield, writer of best seller international books entitled *Peak Performers* and *Second to None.*

Mr. Garfield in his earlier work completed a 15-year study of 1,200 peak performers in every walk of life in the 1980s while a psychology professor at the University of California-San Francisco Medical Center and head of the Peak Performance Center at Berkeley. In regard to this study he said:

> "People who achieve on a high level do seek self-fulfillment, but they also know how to collaborate. They have a good self-image, but are not ego-driven. They have the confidence to solve problems, set attainable goals, and

> take risks to get ahead...High achievers measure themselves against their own standards, not to those of others in the competitive marketplace.... Workaholics...work to compensate for some inadequacy or need in their lives that are not being met. They tend to peak early, then go into a decline or level off."

Dr. George E. Vaillant while at Harvard Medical School revealed the results of a study that began in 1938 on a group of Harvard's best and brightest graduates who went into various walks of life. Dr. Vaillant found that the individuals with the best outcomes were those who could sustain relationships, take long and imaginative vacations, give generously to worthy causes, play competitive sports without assuming a "must win" attitude, and adapt readily to the changes and difficulties of life.

The Harvard Project on Technology, Work, and Character, a nonprofit research organization in Washington, D.C. studied success beginning in the early 1980s, reviewing 250 persons with careers from chief executive to lower level professionals in over 10 large companies. It showed the most trusted and respected managers combined heart qualities (idealism, generosity, courage, and raised consciousness) with head qualities (technical problem solving and practicality).

Warren Bennis, author and co-author of over 20 books, and considered an expert in the field of leadership and power, studied the lives of high achievers over a four-year period while at USC. These individuals had careers as corporate executives, university presidents, public officials, publishers, and winning football coaches. The majority had certain traits in common. They could inspire others, communicate clearly, stay on course regardless of obstacles, learn from mistakes, and improve the performance of their organizations.

What does all this mean for you as an aspirant? Many of the experts believe that a lot of what super-achievers do to make them special is learnable. They believe it is possible to take average people with a high degree of motivation and teach them a general approach to thinking over a period of time that would help them develop performance that would be considered quite exceptional. You can develop your CIFs, you can become a super-achiever, however, my caveat is you must be considered "promotable" in an organization, that is, be a C-1 or C-2 in order to qualify for the competition.

Proficiency levels in the CIFs are critical, however I have also observed another factor that plays a role in the early career successes of African-Americans - geographic origins. My observation is that an unusually high percentage with rural and small town backgrounds spends their careers in C-3. Their strengths are usually high technical competence and good character. This group is taught to be highly technically qualified and practice justice and fair play. They are usually honest, sincere, forthright, less selfish, and go about quietly doing their jobs well. Unfortunately, these characteristics are not highly compensated in the corporate world.

My experience is that as a group, African-Americans from large cities and the West Indies do better in the important earlier years of the corporate environment than do the former category. I have attributed this to them having gained "street smarts" from their formative environments where their survival skills have already been sharpened. Upon entering the organization, during the critical early years, African-Americans from these groups usually communicate better, are more outgoing, seem to be more comfortable in the environment, and are more attuned to the political and competitive dynamics of the corporate world.

A personal example will reinforce the foregoing observations. I grew up in a rural atmosphere. I was very quiet, very technically proficient in my discipline and went about quietly doing my job well. Seventeen years after my electrical engineering undergraduate degree, completion of military training as a commissioned officer and exercising leadership in a combat zone, an MBA, and corporate experience in jobs that had carried the majority to much higher levels, I was stuck in C-3 in the lower echelon of the management ranks.

The integrated oil company I was employed by came under intense takeover pressures in the mid 1980s. I was in the headquarters location in a small town. The company offered an enhanced early retirement package to those over 50 and encouraged many younger professionals of my age with engineering degrees to accept transfers to the plant locations so our talents would be maintained if a takeover attempt were successful.

My division manager, who managed a profit center that generated over $200 million in sales with excellent profits, called me in for a chat after a transfer offer had been extended to me. He was probably in his early 50s and was of European citizenship. My immediate manager reported directly to him and I worked closely with him as the Division Planning and Analysis Specialist. Besides my normal duties in strategic planning, business analysis, budgets and controls, I also prepared materials for his presentations and wrote some of his speeches.

It turned out to be one of the most honest and revealing conversations I have ever had with upper management, sort of "off the record". It was obvious he respected my ability and me. He advised me to take the transfer to the Houston area. If the takeover attempt were successful I would be a lot better off in the larger metropolitan area. And even if the company survived intact but things didn't work out for me at the plant location from a career standpoint, I would have more options and flexibility in Houston than the small town.

We talked to some degree about career fortunes and misfortunes and he indicated how his career had been somewhat fortunate. He had worked with the company's chairman earlier in their careers in Europe and he indicated this had helped him. He indicated that he would take the early retirement and relocate back to Europe.

Nearing the close he said something startling to me. He said, "Lionel, you are too honest." Seeming somewhat surprised by his own forthrightness, he then hastened to clarify himself by calling the company chairman's name and indicating he was not saying the chairman and people at that level were dishonest. He said in order to get to that level you have to say and do certain things. I think I know what he was saying, or at least I have my interpretation. In order to advance up the ladder you have to be a total company person. That often means compromising your personal values and beliefs to display the corporate values and beliefs, albeit they may differ from yours.

I think the following quote from Robert Jackall's article alluded to in Chapter One sums it all up.

> "As it happens, the guidance they (managers) receive from each other is profoundly ambiguous because what matters in the bureaucratic world is not what a person is but how closely his many personae mesh with the organizational ideal; not his willingness to stand by his actions but his agility in avoiding blame; not what he believes or says but how well he has mastered the ideologies that serve his corporation; not what he stands for but whom he stands with in the labyrinths of his organization. In short, bureaucracy structures for managers an intricate series of moral mazes."

In summary, African-Americans are not as prepared in the CIFs as they should be when coming into the career market. While these traits are more innate to some than others, they can be developed and honed. Yet, they must be developed and displayed with a balanced perspective that allows one to relax and maintain a sense of humor. For what good is it to burn out before attaining your goals, or to lose your health in the process?

There must be proactive involvement with young aspirants from key players in order to improve the probabilities of success. Parents who have experience in competitive organizations should provide more preparation to their children in these matters. Colleges need to develop and add courses or segments that focus on the impact of personality, communications and distinction in career development, while continuing to emphasize technical competence. African-Americans need to enter and display to the organization an intensity and sense of urgency, which would improve their CIFs and perhaps lessen the numbers who get assigned to performance C-3 category.

Chapter 4

The Promotions Triangle

Some years later, I developed a different way to look at the "Stairway to Success" model introduced in Chapter 3 and shown in Figures 5 and 6. I shall call this takeoff the Promotions Triangle Theory.

First, some background on its development. One of my African-American coworkers had applied for a promotion to the upper echelon of management in the organization we worked. An African-American from the outside had also applied and was the successful candidate. My coworker had the highest performance rating given by the organization and she should have had the additional advantage of the inside track. Needless to say, she was very disappointed and I asked to provide some feedback to her.

In outlining my points of discussion, I jotted down several key points, and not to my original design, each started with the letter P - performance, promotability, and political connections and/or political expediency. And since models work for me in understanding and presenting concepts, I sketched a triangle with these three Ps as the sides. It is shown in Figure 8. I was able to use the picture as an icebreaker to connect with her for the important conversation that followed. I made some

Figure 8

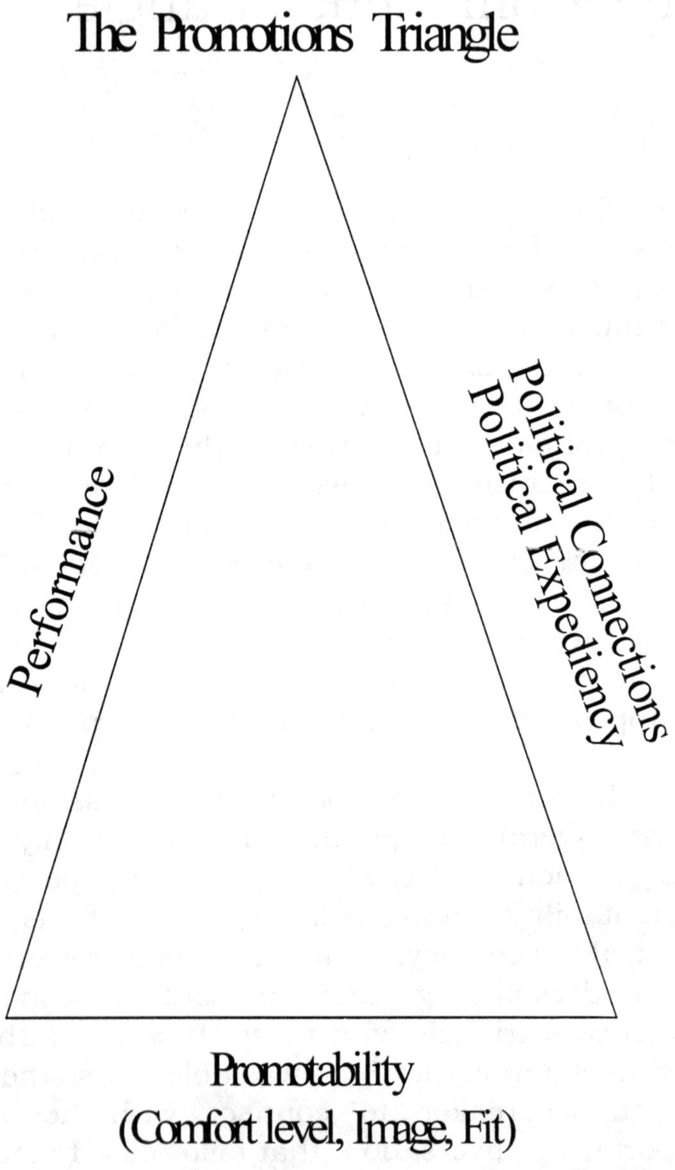
The Promotions Triangle
Performance
Political Connections
Political Expediency
Promotability
(Comfort level, Image, Fit)

remark about my engineering background and my need to see a drawing. It turned out that her ex-husband was an engineer and he had a similar tendency, and fortunately, she didn't tune me out because of the tendency I shared with her ex. I was able to use my triangle sketch to share some of my observations about her methods of candidacy for the position and how I interpreted the organization's process of choosing a candidate to fill the position.

The essence of the model conforms to my basic theme established in the first chapter about promotable people and nonpromotable people in organizations. One's "promotability index" forms the base of the triangle model. It is the foundation from which the other two promotion factors are built and is comprised of the following components; one's image, one's perceived ability to fit in the organization at the level being considered for, and key decision makers' comfort level with the job seeker. It would contain all the elements found in the Figure 6 model starting at the credibility step and going upward to the top. To review, these elements are social and communication skills, personality, distinction, intensity, and sense of urgency.

Performance is the second factor of the model. This would equate with the competence step of the Figure 6 model. As has been stated previously, in many organizations, once certain levels are reached, it is often assumed that the technical competence required to perform a certain job does not vary significantly among the candidates and therefore will not be the primary basis for the decision in the promotions process. And although my coworker had the highest performance rating given by the organization, the decision was not based on her performance only.

The third factor of the model depicts political connections and/or political expediency. Political expediency and political connections are different and both provide significant advantages to its benefactors.

For example, political connections provide significant advantages to the candidates, primarily to those in C-1 described in Chapter One. The characteristic of distinction can also be gained through political connections. Political connections are social and power relationships that have been established by the job seeker him/herself. Persons with these connections have the ability to favorably influence key decision makers and deal makers within and outside the organization. Usually the promotability index will be high. However, their true performance index may not be in the upper percentile of peers.

On the other hand, the decision-makers of the organization use political expediency. Webster's Collegiate Dictionary defines expediency as the quality or state of being suited for the end in view. The following statement can best describe political expediency. **If the organization needs some one for affirmative action goals or to enhance a market or segment appeal, and the organization believes a person of a certain color, gender or national origin will help them achieve the objective, a person will be chosen from the respective group whom the organization believes will best achieve the objective.**

Again, these persons will usually have a high promotability index. However, their true performance index may not be in the upper percentile of peers.

There are three general rules that can be derived using the Promotions Triangle Model that are comparable to the rules resulting from the analysis of the potential versus performance matrix discussed earlier in Figure 2 of Chapter One.

1. Persons with higher performance indexes but lower promotability and political indexes will seldom get promotions to the higher echelon jobs.
2. A higher promotability index will lift the performance index quicker than the reverse. Stated another way, persons with high promotability indexes are usually given higher performance ratings. Therefore, for persons in competition who have the same or similar political expediency/political connections indexes, the person with the higher promotabitlity index will usually get the promotion or position.
3. A higher political expediency/political connections index will lift both the performance and promotability indexes. Stated another way, a person with a higher political index will usually get a higher performance and promotability rating.

Moral of the story: To maximize promotion opportunities, focus on all three Ps of the triangle, recognizing that political connections and/or political expediency will be the factors of distinction.

Chapter 5

Career Plateau: Coming to Grips with the Glass Ceiling

Suppose you are a person with 15 years of experience or less. You have read thus far in the book and can identify with many of the things cited herein. You think you may be at a career plateau but are not sure. Your desires and ambitions are much higher than your current achievements and you are frustrated and angry. Your attitude is not good and all of this is a drag on your performance. You are on the horns of a dilemma. Should you:

- Stay and fight the organization?
- Stay and accept your plight?
- Book flight to another organization?

At this point you need to do a thorough evaluation of your situation. The steps to do this are listed in order below followed by a more detailed analysis.

1. Evaluate the commitment of the organization to you and others like you.
2. Develop the best estimate you can of what you think the organization's assessment of your performance and potential is.

3. Develop your own assessment of your performance and potential.
4. Evaluate the differences in yours and the organization's assessments and determine if these differences can be reconciled.
5. List your life values and priorities.
6. List your life goals and objectives.
7. Evaluate your strengths and weaknesses in relation to the CIFs and positive personal influence factors.
8. Count up the costs - both economical and social.
9. Make your decision after weighing all the relevant factors and receiving input from your "significant other(s)".

A detailed analysis of each step follows:

Step # 1. Thoroughly examine the commitment of your organization to you and others like you. To do this, examine the following:

- Look at the organization's track record. Are there African-Americans at all levels of the management which shows a consistent commitment to hiring, training and promotions over the last 25 years?
- If you do not see African-Americans at all levels, does the management development program include an adequate level of African-American participation?

- Examine management's dialogue on diversity issues. Does management openly acknowledge the concept?
- Are programs in place and functioning that address this issue and are they effective?
- Is there active recruitment of African-American college graduates, especially from predominantly African-American colleges?
- Is there active funding for scholarships and fellowships to African-Americans of more than a token gesture?

Figure 9, "Matrix To Evaluate the Commitment of an Organization", is a model that can be used as a tool to capture your analysis in a central format. It can be used not only to analyze your current organization, but also in studying an organization under your consideration. The rating of the answers on a scale of 1-10 to the foregoing questions under Step #1 would fall along the X-axis. The Y-axis, "Ability to Attract", would include a plot of the ratings on a scale of 1-10 of factors about the company such as the following:

- Pay and benefits
- Amenities and office environment
- Location
- Commitment to the community
- Family friendly issues
- Other issues important to attract and retain you

The higher and to the right these factors are, the more favorable the organization. So a company that

Figure 9

Matrix to Evaluate the Commitment of an Organization

Ability to Attract

Higher Ability Lower Commitment Q-2	Higher Ability Higher Commitment Q-3
Lower Ability Lower Commitment Q-1	Lower Ability Higher Commitment Q-4

Commitment to Equal Opportunity

plotted in Q-3 would be ideal, followed by companies that plotted in Q-2 and Q-4. Obviously, an organization that plotted in Q-1 would be very unattractive to you.

Step # 2. Develop the best estimate you can of what you think the organization's estimate of your career outlook is. This will be a difficult but not an impossible task. You must begin by plotting your performance/potential matrix as in Figure 2.

- You must talk to various people including coworkers, current and former managers, and any others you think may share some information on your performance, and/or the organization's evaluation system. You should include those people whom you think are sympathetic to your situation because they will usually be more willing to share a certain amount of the needed information with you.
- You should be aware of the criteria for determining performance. This should have been understood at the beginning of your entrance into the organization. If you don't know, find out now. This is usually commonly shared information. What you need to know are the specific performance ratings and/or words that are used to identify the various percentiles of the employee population, particularly the top 25 percent. If you are not in this league, the foregoing information has already told you where you stand and what it means to you.

At a company I worked, the top 25th percentile performers got ratings of superior and highly competent.

- You also need to know your potential rating or promotability index. This rating has to do with their assessment of the timing and maximum achievable grade you are thought to attain within the organization. Companies do this differently but the results are the same. You have been assigned some kind of evaluator, perhaps in code form, consisting of a number or a word, which says one of the following; you are capable of advancing X number of grade levels above where you are now, you are capable of reaching a certain numbered grade level, or you are capable of reaching low, middle or upper management positions. This information is more difficult to get than that of performance. In the Texaco case referred to earlier which hit the press in 1996, Texaco had used secret lists to designate which employees had the potential to be senior executives. If you cannot find anyone in your chain of command that will share this type of information with you (many won't), you can get some good indications on what the company thinks of you by looking at those persons now that you considered your peers when you first came into the organization. For example, if a peer has had two or three promotions in 5 years and you have had none or one, this is a good indication that you are probably C-3 (potential rated lower) versus their C-1/C-2 (potential rated higher). If after 7-10 years, a peer has reached middle management and you are still down at the lower levels, you are in Quadrant 1 or 4 versus them being in Quadrant 2 or 3. Refer to the discussion about Figure 2 for the implications about those in the various quadrants.

Step # 3. Realistically evaluate your assessment of your performance and potential and plot this on the matrix, Figure 2.

Step # 4. Evaluate the difference between the company's assessment and your assessment. If you have yourself in Quadrant 2 or 3 and you think they have you in Quadrant 1 or 4, there will probably be no reconciliation and little hope for a change in status. There may, however, be some opportunity to move further out along the performance axis from Quadrant 1 to Quadrant 4 on the company's assessment, that is, to change their perception of your performance.

Following is a situation analysis of each quadrant in Figure 2 along with some personal strategies, which should help you with Steps 1, 2, 3 and 4 of the personal evaluation process:

SITUATION ANALYSIS CASE #1

LOCATION: Quadrant 1, Category 3.
DEFINITION: Lower performance, Lower potential.
STATE OF AFFAIRS: Cautious balance.
COMPANY SAYS: Be a good soldier.
RESULTS: Raises nil or below average, promotions nil, jobs as accountants, analysts, and engineers.

KEY FACTORS TO IMPROVE:

Current perception of quality and quantity of work.
Building consensus among key decision-makers and influentials.

PERSONAL STRATEGIES:

Identify the perceived or actual performance criteria being used to rate you.
Identify the potential characteristics being used to determine advancement.
Identify which of the CIFs you need improvement in.
Do you have the ability and motivation to improve?
How much will it cost you in time, effort, and money?
What is the payoff?
Cost/benefits ratio?
Decision: Plight, fight, or flight.

SITUATION ANALYSIS CASE # 2

LOCATION:	Quadrant 2, Category 2.
DEFINITION:	Higher potential, medium to lower performance.
STATE OF AFFAIRS:	Good but not great.
COMPANY SAYS:	Performing at lower than expected performance.
ULTIMATE JOBS:	Department manager, division manager.

KEY FACTORS TO IMPROVE:

Perception of current performance.
Sphere of influence.

PERSONAL STRATEGIES:

Identify the performance factors in the current job that need improvement.
Do you have the ability and motivation to improve?
Revitalize or redefine your existing mentor relationship or seek a new mentor.
Build support with those who rate and approve your rating (if these are not your mentors), and with those who provide input on your performance rating.
Initiate an action plan.

SITUATION ANALYSIS CASE # 3

LOCATION:	Quadrant 3, Categories 1& 2
DEFINITION:	Higher performance, higher potential.
STATE OF AFFAIRS:	Bright.
COMPANY SAYS:	You are going places.
RESULTS:	Raises above average, excellent visibility and exposure, changing jobs with increasing responsibility and/or promotions every 18-36 months, being trained in key areas of the organization.
ULTIMATE JOBS:	Vice president and above.

KEY FACTORS TO IMPROVE:

Sphere of influence.
Leadership skills.
Articulate the organization's vision.

PERSONAL STRATEGIES:

Hone CIFs.
Develop networks and alliances.
Broaden sphere of influence.
Continue to insure that current performance is perceived to be excellent.

SITUATION ANALYSIS CASE # 4

LOCATION:	Quadrant 4, Category 3 or low Category 2.
DEFINITION:	Higher performance, lower potential.
STATE OF AFFAIRS:	Acceptable to satisfactory.
COMPANY SAYS:	Not suitable for higher responsibility.
RESULTS:	Raises are average, with stagnation or slow progress on the technical ladder or lower supervision ladder. Promotion to the next highest grade occurs 8-12 years apart with one or at best two more before retirement.

KEY FACTORS TO IMPROVE:

Sphere of influence.
Building consensus among key decision-makers and influentials.

PERSONAL STRATEGIES:

Identify the potential characteristics being stated as a prerequisite for advancement.
Determine why your potential is rated lower and can it be changed at this point in your career.

Are the reasons within your control? You cannot change your age, race or sex and although one may be the real reason for your stagnation, management will not admit it and you may not be able to prove it.
Do you have the ability and motivation to improve?
How much will it cost you in time, effort, and money?
What is the payoff?
Cost/benefits ratio?
Decision: Plight, fight, or flight.

Step # 5. Determine your values and priorities.

Before proceeding, I should define values and priorities and how they should be used in this personal planning process. A value is a personal quality or trait that you have or desire, or a principle that you strive to live by that you believe brings personal satisfaction, harmony and meaning to your life. A priority is a decision, usually followed by actions, to place one thing in front of, or on top of another due to its urgency or importance to you. Therefore, values help you establish, guide and maintain your actions (priorities). Succinctly establishing values and priorities helps one allocate his/her personal resources, both from an urgency (timing) and importance (consequence) standpoint, because we usually don't have all the personal resources (money, talent, time) to accomplish our objectives simultaneously.

Values are personal, therefore, priorities usually differ among individuals and households. And, if you don't have any values and priorities, or haven't clarified them, you will be working from those of someone else.

There are always tradeoffs and choices where values and priorities are the driving forces and these choices are always made, either consciously or unconsciously. Some examples of these tradeoffs would include:

- Career versus family
- Career versus personal health
- Financial wants versus financial needs
- Employee wants versus employer wants
- Social wants versus personal wants

Before one can properly set goals and objectives, s/he must give careful consideration to identify and clarify his/her values. We all have them and live by them, however, most of us have never really sought to bring them into sharper focus and commit them to paper. Therefore, to aid in this endeavor, two lists have been prepared that can help you clarify and articulate your values - one list for personal values and another for work values, which are shown in Appendix A and B respectively. The items on these lists will have varying levels of importance to you and are not all-inclusive, so please add other values that you honor.

Your first task is to carefully study each list. After doing this, you may want to add to the lists in columns one some of your own additional important work and personal values. Your next task for each list is to identify in column two each value in terms of High (H), Medium (M), or Low (L). Your final task in column three is to determine your five highest values, in descending order, starting with a rating of five for your highest value.

Once this process is completed, your highest values should help you determine which life goals and objectives you will seek and the ranking should help you establish the urgency and importance of the actions you will pursue in attaining these goals and objectives.

Step # 6. List your life goals and objectives.

The difficult task of identifying and acknowledging what you really want out of life can only be done by asking yourself some hard questions and giving yourself honest answers. If you have never made a systematic effort to do this before, now is an excellent time. The personal planning process should encompass a period of at least 10-25 years into the future and should cover the following key aspects of your life; spiritual, mental, physical and economic. I believe you can get a sense of urgency and importance of this task by asking yourself this very penetrating question. If my employing organization planned its future the way I plan for my family's future, would I have the income and benefits I have?

With the above perspective, you should now be in a mindset to take this task seriously. To make the task more focused, your personal plan should be broken down into the areas of financial, family, social, spiritual, health and intellectual. First determine your goal for each area, that is, the destination you desire in 10-25 years. Secondly, back up to the present and set a five year objective for each area. The objective should be SMART: (specific, measurable, attainable, relevant, and timed). Thirdly, you and your family or significant other(s) should do a value analysis to help you set the priorities for the objectives you decide to seek. The forth step in this process is to set one year objectives for each category followed by a set of action plans that are necessary and that you plan to take to complete each objective. Action plans are tasks and activities that support the achievement of each objective.

For your reference and guide in preparing your plan, the personal planning process is outlined in Appendix C.

As part of your plan under financial, you should address how a move to another organization may help bring this goal into fruition. Here are some key questions to consider:

1. Based on my experience and training, what kinds of tasks and activities do I enjoy most? Enjoy least?
2. If I could have any job, which would it be? Why? Is this the ultimately desired job?
3. How important are factors such as income, location, job security, job travel, independence and autonomy, advancement, and the type of company and industry?
4. What price am I willing to pay to achieve my desired job goal?

5. How far up the corporate ladder do I want to ascend?

Step # 7. Evaluate your personal strengths and weaknesses.

The next major step in analyzing whether a career move would help you achieve your personal goals and objectives is to evaluate your strengths and weaknesses. The degree to which you can change some of the items you identify will vary. However, your aim is to capitalize and maximize your strengths, and mitigate or eliminate your weaknesses. The evaluation should start with these questions:

1. Based on my experience and training, what are my six strongest skills? Skills would encompass such things as computer programming, teaching and training, mentoring, cost accounting, and management acumen, etc.
2. What have been my three greatest accomplishments in life? Which are repeatable?
3. Why should an employer hire and promote me?

Next, rate yourself on the characteristics listed below using a scale of:

-2 = Much poorer than peers
-1 = Poorer than peers
0 = Equal to peers

+1 = Better than peers
+2 = Much better than peers

Here are the characteristics under the categories of achievements and ability, career influence factors, and personal positive influence (described in the next chapter). To be more meaningful, you should list more specific subcategories under these main headings where appropriate:

Achievements and Ability

______Educational credentials
______Professional certification
______Professional awards and recognition
______Leadership ability
______Administrative knowledge and ability
______Creativity and ingenuity

Career Influence Factors (CIFs)

______Technical skills
______Communications skills
______Personality and social skills
______Distinction
______Sense of urgency
______Intensity

Personal Positive Influence

______Good looks
______Dress and grooming
______Ability to encourage and compliment

Thirdly, go through and pick out your five greatest strengths and decide if you have any distinctive strengths. A distinctive strength would be a personal or skill attribute unique to you, or which you have that is rarely found among your peers. A rating on any of the above of +2 (much better than peers), would suggest that this is a distinctive strength. For your greatest strengths, write down all the benefits you believe will accrue to any employer through you.

Next, review and develop plans to deal with your weaknesses. A weakness is any item you rated yourself a (-1) or (-2). Determine if any of your weaknesses are fixed. For example, shyness, a subcategory under personality, may be considered a fixed weakness. Develop an action plan to mitigate any of those weaknesses. For the other weaknesses that are not considered fixed, develop action plans to eliminate or mitigate them as well. Finally, go over your evaluation with a trusted family member or friend and ask for, and be open to honest feedback.

Step #8. Count up the costs - both economical and social.

It is now time to compare the personal cost to you of whether to accept the plight, stay and fight or, book flight to another organization. You have done all the analyses in Steps 1-7. Now these must be summed to a conclusion looking at both economic and social factors. Economic costs include all costs to achieve the financial goals and objectives you desire. Social factors include geographic ties and uprooting children and spouse to name a few.

Situation Analysis # 5 will provide a systematic method to do this.

Step # 9. Make your decision after weighing all the above relevant factors and receiving input from your significant other(s).

The foregoing nine-step process is designed as a proactive approach to help put certain key things in perspective. An honest personal assessment will equip you to identify realities and the personal plan will provide you a road map to help you secure a more meaningful life and career.

Our last case analysis will be one of a "confirmed" career plateau. This case is designed to help you apply Steps 5-9 of the evaluation process in dealing with a career plateau issue.

SITUATION ANALYSIS # 5

GOAL: You have a goal of middle management and higher.

SCENARIO: You think you have the CIFs, and have performed at a level commensurate with peers who have left you standing still in a staff or lower supervisory level. You've been with the company for over 10 years.

DECISION TIME: Fight, flight, or plight.

REALIZATIONS TO ACKNOWLEDGE:

Your performance and /or potential are probably rated lower.

If you are over forty, you are probably not going any higher than one, or perhaps two more grades.

Institutional and / or personal racism and discrimination may have contributed to your circumstances. Your task to overcome this obstacle is formidable, if not insurmountable.

You will be fighting tradition, inertia, and the corporate culture.

GREATEST NEED:

A commitment from the organization.

PERSONAL ACTION PLAN:

Evaluate your strengths and weaknesses.

Evaluate your CIFs.

Evaluate what you want from your job or career.

Review your options.

Count up the costs in view of all the factors listed earlier.

Decision: Change jobs, fight, or accept plight.

For the person who thinks s/he faces this situation, do not allow your frustration with your current predicament to cloud your forward thinking and planning. The major criterion for evaluating a career opportunity should be to the extent it helps you achieve your life goals, both short and long term. It is important to look past the next job if your goal is upward mobility. You can now begin to focus on specific actions toward your objectives. This includes not only job offers with promotion potential outside your current organization, but also internal transfer possibilities and developmental activities such as company training, or returning to school to enhance your skills or to gain new skills.

Career opportunities should be evaluated by considering a variety of job related issues such as the:

- Whole economy
- Labor market in general and for your specific skills
- Industry, including its health and lifecycle
- Company, including its culture and image
- Specific division or department within the company
- Specific job opportunity in consideration

Remember from our discussion in Chapter Two, certain departments and jobs have a higher value to the company than others and this is reflected in the type of people selected to fill those positions. Therefore, the following information should be gathered and considered very carefully before a decision is made to venture into a new situation:

- Important trends in the prospective industry and company
- Reputation of the company
- Reputation, importance and status of the department where the prospective job is

- Financial contribution of the department
- Value of the prospective job as a step to a higher position for you
- Importance of the prospective job to the organization
- Characteristics of peers and managers in the department

To help analyze a prospective job, I have developed a list of many of the aforementioned factors grouped under several headings. The first group is called Personal Considerations. Column A of the list deals with reality issues such as values, priorities, goals, etc, which you have previously decided (or should decide) will govern your life. This column also includes some additional key factors such as age, health and family lifecycle. Column B, Personal Satisfaction, addresses the level of personal satisfaction you have with your geographic location, community involvement, lifestyle, etc.

Personal Considerations

Column A **Personal Realities**	**Column B** **Personal Satisfaction**
Values	Lifestyle
Priorities	Leisure time
Life Goals/objectives	Community Involvement
Age	Spiritual Enrichment
Years of Service	Geographical Preferences & Ties
Health	Financial Condition
Family Life Cycle	

The second grouping includes a review of the characteristics, trends and potential in the companies as well as the industries you are considering. The lists are as follows:

Industry and Company Characteristics

Column A - Industry	**Column B - Company**
Structure	Position in industry
Profitability	Financial strength
Growth prospects	Growth potential
Economic cycles	Management style
Technological changes	Company policies
Potential to achieve goals	Potential to achieve goals

The third and final grouping addresses what I call the rewards (Column A), and demands/deficiencies (Column B) of the job alternatives themselves. The lists are not all- inclusive. You should add other factors that may apply to your specific situation.

Job Considerations

Rewards	**Demands / Deficiencies**
Location	Stress Levels
Advancement Potential	Travel
Independence and challenge	Job pressures
Ability to meet career goals	Work hours
Job Satisfaction	Work Atmosphere
Job Enrichment	Lack Organizational Commitment
Pay/Benefits	
Status	
Amenities	

This particular analysis can be shown as quantitative results by rating each factor on a scale of 1-10 and plotting the results on Figure 10, "Matrix to Evaluate a Move Decision." The personal consideration and job consideration factors should be evaluated and plotted for both the current job and the new job and organization under consideration.

The demands the organization places on you should be plotted along the X-axis inversely. That is, the higher the demand or greater the deficiency, the lower the rating or score it should receive, and visa versa.

The job rewards and the personal satisfaction factors should be plotted along the Y-axis. The higher the numerical value given to the reward or contentment factor, the greater the satisfaction should be to you.

Figure 11 shows the table results printed within the respective quadrants of the evaluation matrix. The quadrant with the greatest number of points suggest the decision to be made. However, a mere numerical score may not give you the best answer since factors you are attempting to chart may have different weights depending on your personal realities (values, priorities, etc.). You should be aware of this since our example assumes all factors have the same weights.

The following two tables show the values plotted in Figure 11. This is an example of an individual who is considering leaving a position after 10 years with a company. Only the current employer's factors are shown here. The personal realities should be considered in your analysis but are not given a numerical rating. You should have already thoroughly evaluated these issues which now will establish and guide your decision making process.

Personal Considerations

Personal Realities	X-axis Not plotted	Personal Satisfaction	Y-axis
Values		Lifestyle	7
Priorities		Leisure time	7
Life Goals/objectives		Community involvement	3
Age		Spiritual enrichment	6
Years of Service		Geographical preferences	7
Health		Financial position	7
Family Life Cycle			

Job Considerations

Rewards	Y-axis	Demands & Deficiencies	X-axis
Location	6	Stress levels	3
Advancement potential	1	Lack organizational commitment	2
Job satisfaction	3	Job pressures	6
Job enrichment	4	Work hours	7
Pay & benefits	7	Work atmosphere	6
Status	3	Travel	9
Amenities	4		

The example suggests a "stay" mode, Quadrant 3. A review of the charting in Figure 11 indicates Quadrant 3 has 75 points (47 for the Y factors and 28 for the X factors). Please note that the Y factors are directly proportional, the higher the points, the higher the attractiveness; whereas the X factors are inversely proportional, the higher the demand or greater the deficiency, the lower the points.

Figure 10

Matrix to Evaluate a Move Decision

Job Rewards and Personal Satisfaction

Higher Job Rewards Higher Personal Satisfaction Unfavorable Job Demands **DECISION: EITHER** Q-2	Higher Job Rewards Higher Personal Satisfaction Favorable Job Demands **DECISION: STAY** Q-3
Lower Job Rewards Lower Personal Satisfaction Unfavorable Job Demands **DECISION: GO** Q-1	Lower Job Rewards Lower Personal Satisfaction Favorable Job Demands **DECISION: EITHER** Q-4

Job Demands

Figure 11

Example of a Move Evaluation

10

Higher Y factors		Lower X factors	
Spiritual enrichment	6	Lack commitment	2
Financial position	7	Stress levels	3
Geographical ties	7		
Leisure time	7		
Pay/benefits	7		
Lifestyle	7		
Location	6		
	47		5

EITHER---2

Higher Y factors		Higher X factors	
Spiritual enrichment	6	Work atmosphere	6
Financial position	7	Job pressures	6
Geographical ties	7	Work hours	7
Leisure time	7	Travel	9
Pay/benefits	7		
Lifestyle	7		
Location	6		
	47		28

STAY---3

5

Lower Y factors		Lower X factors	
Community involve.	3	Lack commitment	2
Advance potential	1	Stress levels	3
Job satisfaction	3		
Job enrichment	4		
Amenities	4		
Status	3		
	18		5

GO--1

Lower Y factors		Higher X factors	
Community involve.	3	Work atmosphere	6
Advance potential	1	Job pressures	6
Job satisfaction	3	Work hours	7
Job enrichment	4	Travel	9
Amenities	4		
Status	3		
	18		28

EITHER---4

0 5 10

Epilog

In closing this chapter, several terms that I used should be defined to insure the points are well understood:

Family Life Cycle: This term refers to the makeup and the stage in the family's development. Is the family; one or two career, childless or empty nest, or single parent or both parents? The values and priorities will be different because of the makeup and stage of development and all of the relationship dynamics that take place surrounding these.

Lifestyle: This refers to the types and pace of activities and entertainment one is involved in outside work. Some may be busy most nights and weekend away from their place of residence, whereas, others may concentrate on home based activities, while others may operate somewhere in between.

Job Enrichment: The variety and complexity of challenges and activities within a job that allows one the flexibility to use his/her judgement, skills, experience and creative abilities to get greater personal satisfaction and productivity.

Status: The amount of personal self esteem felt as a result of being part of the organization or being in the job position.

Company policies: Policies regarding career development such as – Is the culture geared toward sink or swim, or training and development? Is there transfer between line and staff positions?

Characteristics of managers and peers: What is the length of time these persons have been in their positions and what are their ages? How competitive are your potential peers and what are their competencies? Are the higher levels filled by managers not promotable or waiting for retirement?

Chapter 6

Sources of Personal Positive Influence

You have read some things that have raised your interest and caused you to act or contemplate action. Regardless of your decision of fight, flight or plight, the rest of the book will provide you with additional insights and techniques that can help you whatever your choice.

I introduced the phrase "personal positive influence" (PPI) in Step 7 of the previous chapter. The focus of this chapter is to define and identify several sources of it that can be developed or enhanced to increase one's sphere of influence. I mentioned in Chapter 3 that all of us influence either positively or negatively. Personal positive influence is the power (ability) to influence others positively using personal attributes. One certain way for the 80 percent of African-Americans who are in C-3 to improve their progress in the management hierarchy is to exert more positive influence.

It is important to distinguish between the two basic sources of power for the individual - personal and position. As the name implies, personal power comes from personal attributes such as physical stature, knowledge and skills, communication ability, and character. Position power comes by virtue of the authority granted to a person by a sovereign entity in which he/she resides or operates, i.e., being the governor of a state, president of a company or pastor of a church. Therefore, personal power is evoked through a personal attribute or ability and position power is evoked through the rights granted by a sovereign entity. Used properly, both can be used to create an edge, however my focus is on the personal power.

These sources of PPI that I will touch on briefly have been thoroughly discussed and written about. Libraries are replete with information. You should go to other books and references on the specific areas of interest. My objective is to reinforce the importance of these factors and make you aware of things that may not have been considered heretofore, things that can have a real impact on a career.

However, before I proceed, I must turn aside and stress a key point. That is, almost anything can be counterfeited. The same goes with these sources of personal positive influence. They should be developed and used to enhance your impact and not used to manipulate others.

Beauty and Attractiveness (Good Looks)

One of the first things noticed about a person is his/her physical appearance such as the attractiveness of the features and the height. Although there are certain aspects about our appearance we cannot change, an awareness of how we as humans respond to each other based on such attributes can help us maximize the benefits of those features, or minimize the negative perceptions and responses.

Studies have proven what our personal experiences have told us all our lives - attractive and taller people of both sexes receive far more positive feedback and advantages. Physical attributes are a definite source of personal positive influence. Research conducted in the late 1970s by Elaine Hatfield at the University of Wisconsin showed that from the third grade onward, attractive people would usually get the benefit of the doubt. Both men and women perceive beautiful people as smarter, warmer, more moral and more prone to success. Ms Hatfield later co-authored a book entitled *Mirror, Mirror the Importance of Looks in Everyday Life.*

A more recent study released in 1997 by the National Bureau of Economic Research, a nonprofit research foundation, and reported in the Wall Street Journal, suggests good-looking people generate more money for their employers than their plain co-workers. Another report by the foundation showed the more attractive earn higher wages than the less attractive. Other studies have shown that taller men earn more than shorter men do in similar jobs by at least $1000 per inch per year.

What does all this mean for you, the aspirant? If these studies have any truth, and our personal experiences can attest that they do, then attractive persons can have an advantage - a distinction that can help separate them from the crowd. If the attractive and/or taller person adds value to the organization by bringing a real or perceived increase in clients, improved customer service, or a more pleasant atmosphere, this would translate directly to the bottom line through increased productivity or revenues. Then, it stands to reason the person providing this value-added should be rewarded with favorable treatment that may include upward mobility and promotions within the organization.

Dress and Grooming

In conjunction with natural physical appearance, dress and grooming are other visual factors that can provide a source of PPI. There are numerous studies and books on the subject of dressing for success and power dressing. Those who have a special interest should study this subject in more detail.

The truth of the matter is what you wear in important settings can make or break you. Your clothes can be your best friend or worst enemy. Many psychotherapists agree that around 90 percent of what people remember about an encounter are through nonverbal communications. Your dress and grooming convey nonverbal clues about your personality, education, background, and financial position. These clues can break down barriers and launch careers or create barriers and stifle careers.

Experts also tell us that textures, types of materials and even the cut lines in the clothing transmit silent messages. A soft texture in attire is said tends to invite human contact and closeness while crisp textures may suggest that a person wants to be regarded as efficient. Strict or flowing lines are said to provide some indication of the rigidity of one's personality. And in many instances clothes are the only visible clues to our personality.

Your skills at sending and interpreting the visual code of dress makes a great difference in your ability to influence and relate to others. And just as sure as you get impressions of others from their dress and grooming, always be cognizant that others are getting impressions of you. For better or worse, realize that your outward appearance influences how others will react and respond to you. By emphasizing the positive aspects of yourself through dress and grooming, you can inspire confidence in your skills and abilities, and create more positive influence.

Compliments and Encouragement

Lastly, another source of PPI can come through the ability to compliment and encourage others. Words of appreciation and praise both enrich and enhance our lives. A positive approach in both the business and personal life pays off in productivity and an improved environment; and while words of appreciation motivates others, they also make our lives richer. We all like to run compliments through our minds again and again and they serve as an anecdote against the times we feel low.

Someone once noted that big businesses and corporations spend millions of dollars on advertising their products and services and neglect the one thing that both customers and employees really respond to - appreciation. It is worthwhile to note that since the early 90s big business has realized this and placed a greater emphasis on better customer service. Although the motive is profit rather than altruistic, this is still a welcomed change.

Mark Twain was attributed to have said, " I can live for two months on a good compliment." The sad fact is most of us guard our compliments and encouragement of others as if they were some private treasure.

In business, supervisors and managers are prompted to provide “constructive criticism” of employees. However, I remember hearing my business school professor of organization and management say there is no such thing as “constructive criticism.” His implication was that all criticism is destructive. I believe there is a lot of truth in his statement. Similarly, I remember a quote I read somewhere that said, “ Correction accomplishes much, compliments accomplish much more.”

If we accept the fact that the appreciation or compliment donor - that is - the originator does reap positive benefits as well as the receiver, how can we learn to do it more effectively? There are several keys for expressing effective appreciation; frequency, timing, sincerity, and sensitivity. The first keys are frequency and timing - say appreciative words more often.

Also, the proper timing will add to the meaning. Most people expect and often receive compliments during certain situations, such as when an excellent presentation was made or much sought-after new account was obtained. However when subordinates, coworkers, friends, or family members have tried hard but missed the mark, didn't get approval during the presentation or didn't close the much-sought deal, give them credit for their dedicated and gallant effort. Where there is praise there is usually second and third effort.

The next key for becoming more effective in providing compliments is sincerity. Avoid empty flattery. It is better not to say anything than to be dishonest. Dale Carnegie observed, “Flattery is from the teeth out, appreciation is from the heart out.” Carnegie knew “how to win friends and influence people.” The sincerity of the praise is authenticated when the individual has control over the object of the praise. For example, when complimenting an individual, personality and character traits may be better choices than outward appearance or apparel, especially in the office environment when dealing with the opposite sex, because of sexual harassment issues.

Compliments also improve the correction process by accentuating the positive. I once read a story of a manager who had a secretary who did excellent work while displaying an excellent attitude and personality, but who was slow in her typing speed. Instead of the manager saying, “You do excellent work and you have a great attitude and personality but your typing is slow”, he said, “You’re the most accurate typist who has ever worked for me and if you typed faster, you’d be the best secretary I’ve ever known”. This choice of wording gave the secretary the motivation to improve her speed, which she did, and she did become one of the best secretaries the manager had ever known. As the manager moved up, she moved up with him.

Notice the use of the phrase “and if you typed faster” rather than “but your typing is slow.” Try to avoid the use of the word “but” except maybe in a debate. It carries a negative connotation that usually cancels out the benefits of anything positive said before. The conjunction "and" usually works as well or better. And also, as we recall from personal experience, we don't often change just because someone points out our faults. There must be an incentive.

Compliments are also more effective when directed at persons rather than things. Instead of saying "Maurice, that was an excellent report," say "Maurice, you did a great job in capturing all the vital information in your report in an accurate, clear, and concise manner."

Compliments can be written or spoken. A handwritten note of praise on a memo or report will usually be retained long after many similar items are discarded. A timely personal note of thanks or appreciation on your personal stationery or card stock in your own personal handwriting is far more valued than a typed version. The personal touch is also preferred over the computer scanned personal handwriting and signature.

The Houston Chronicle daily newspaper in its June 24, 2000 edition reported results on a recent study that said praise is a key way to motivate staff. The paper indicated Gerald Graham of Wichita State University studied more than 1,500 employees in scores of work settings. The top one and two motivators were:

1. The manager personally congratulating employees who did a good job, and
2. The manager writing personal notes about good performance.

The final principle in becoming more effective in expressing appreciation is learning to be more sensitive. Pay more attention to the people, actions and activities around you. Tune in your sensory perception to the wants and needs of others. "Your own success can depend on your sensitivity to others;" writes Bernard Gittelson in his book *How To Make Your Own Luck*. I think the Bible in Proverbs 25:11 (KJV) says it well, " A word fitly spoken is like apples of gold in pictures of silver."

Chapter 7

Skills That Enhance Your PPI

Not only do the foregoing attributes of good looks, smart dress and grooming, and the ability to compliment and encourage others contribute to a PPI, the following abilities and skills can help as well to promote a PPI and contribute to success:

Selling skills

I once read a statement that said the whole world is in sales. There is a lot of truth in the statement. From our youth up we have been selling ourselves and our ideas. At home we had to sell our parents on giving us an allowance, going out for the team, having a slumber party, borrowing the car, or going out on a date. In marriage, social, community and business settings, we have to sell our ideas and proposals.

Most professionals in business have numerous opportunities each year to sell themselves and their ideas and proposals to their immediate superiors, those higher in the chain, and other influential persons. But unfortunately, most opportunities are overlooked or misused. Although some fall into your lap, more often you must create them yourself. First, you must learn to recognize what occasions can be used as opportunities and begin to showcase your management skills as those opportunities are presented or created.

To advance in an organization, it is often necessary to tell decision-makers what a good job you are doing. It is not enough in many companies just to do a good job and hope that someone notices and appreciates it. Particularly in the larger organization, those in authority do not necessarily know what you have done for them lately. Active evidence is what you need, and it works.

Some common occasions that can be turned into valuable opportunities to sell yourself include the following:

Performance Reviews: Many organizations have these on a regular basis as I referred earlier. You should be highly prepared to demonstrate not only your accomplishments, but also the decision making and problem solving techniques you used to complete your assignments. Most professionals and managers loathe this occasion and therefore most professionals fail to take full advantage of its potential to highlight their skills. Think of performance reviews as opportunities rather than challenges.

If your organization does not have a formal process, you should design a method whereby you provide your superior a weekly progress report, preferably in person, with a more in-depth monthly report. Further, you should request a quarterly or semiannual meeting with your direct superior to formulate tasks and assignments, set goals and objectives, review progress, and identify challenges and opportunities. You should keep good documentation of the dialogues, and preferably, write a memo to your boss summarizing the key points and conclusions from these meetings.

Finding an Advocate and Giving Him/Her Ammunition To Sell You: Your advocate could be your immediate supervisor or someone else in management interested in helping you. Depending on your relationship, you may have to wait for the most opportune time to come forth with the accomplishments you want to be carried forward. Again, look for those noteworthy situations to highlight your management skills to your advocate. S/he wants your best ammunition to sell you so be specific about the techniques and methodology you used in getting the results you got.

Formal Meetings and Reports: These can be meetings or reports that you initiate or those that are already a part of your job or company's standard operating procedures such as:

- Forecasts
- Recommendations
- Progress reports on important projects
- Requests for operating or capital budget appropriations
- Changes in policies and procedures in human resources, purchasing, etc
- Internal newsletters and communications

In all these instances, it is important to emphasize why you recommend a specific solution or why you reached the conclusion you reached. Outlining the steps you took highlights your judgment, decision making and systematic planning skills.

Another way to highlight your skills is to ask for advice or feedback on progress you have already made. You might try stating it this way, "This is how we (I) have handled the project so far. These are the steps that have been taken and these are the reasons for this approach. What ideas do you have to help us (me) maximize the outcome?" This approach depicts you as a forward thinking person with keen interpersonal awareness and good systematic planning skills.

One final point. You may feel uncomfortable about describing not only what you have accomplished, but also the why and wherefore, because you think the technique can be overused or be seen as self-promoting. The fact is, however, that most of your proposals and recommendations can only be "sold" by showing the logic and thinking behind them. A good manager will challenge your assumptions and if you can defend them well, most of the battle of selling your solution or recommendation is won. I believe it is far better to take the initiative during your presentation, time and circumstances permitting, and spell out the process to your conclusion or recommendation. This helps the decision-makers evaluate your solutions better.

Decision Making Skills

In selling, we are trying to persuade others to our way of thinking or even convince them our idea is the best one. Any way you look at it, we want the other person to make a decision in our favor, that is, to say "yes." Likewise, other persons ask the same from you. That is, s/he wants you to make a decision. Therefore, good decision making skills are important for a successful life and management career.

In making decisions, usually there is some amount of fear. It is this fear that prevents many from achieving their objectives in life. It must be understood there is fear on both sides of the equation - fear for you and the person you approach - whether that person is a prospect, a client/customer, a superior, or a family member.

A theory in an article written by Jimmy Cabrera suggests this fear is shared 50 / 50 between each of you. Because of your new-found knowledge, you are aware the approached party is afraid, but s/he doesn't necessarily know that you are afraid. Therefore, remember, you should always have the advantage.

The theory analyzes fear as follows: Notice the word F**EA**R and the two middle letters, E and A.

> **E:** The approached person is hesitant to **E**nter into or make a decision.
> Why: The fear of making a wrong decision.
>
> **A:** You are hesitant to **A**sk for the decision.
> Why: The fear of rejection or failure.

The mind consists of the conscious and the subconscious. Our experiences define what is in our minds, and 90 percent of our actions are controlled by our subconscious mind according to Cabrera.

Let's analyze this a bit further. We have made hundreds of thousands of decisions in our lifetime and how we made decisions yesterday and yesteryear affect the way we make decisions today. You see, since we first started to make decisions as toddlers, the consequences of those decisions are registered in our subconscious. You may be twenty something, forty something or sixty something, and have made many decisions. But ask yourself this question, Do you think in your subconscious there are more profound memories of the negative consequences, or of the positive consequences, of your past decisions? If there are more memories of negative consequences, you will likely be more averse to decision making and your fear factor will be higher.

During a presentation, you ask me to make a major decision. It could be in reference to a product, service, or policy. If my subconscious is more pain oriented (more memories of the negative consequences of my decisions), what kinds of thoughts and feelings will emerge in my conscious mind? Fear, loathe. Therefore, I will be more averse to making a decision and will attempt to avoid it.

I believe the foregoing theory helps to put the decision-making dilemma in perspective. A heightened awareness of the two sides of fear should increase the desire to hone your skills, and in addition, increase your compassion and empathy for others you approach for decisions. Certainly, more information enhances the decision making process by increasing knowledge which reduces fear, so focus on providing as much relevant information as possible in your transactions that require others to make decisions - whether business or personal.

We can also improve our chances of getting to "yes" by being more skilled in reading the verbal and nonverbal cues of the other person during this process of interaction. This allows us to better manage the interactive process and provide the proper responses to overcome the reluctance or objection and close the "sale". This skill can be enhanced through the study of personality types.

So far I have talked about success through decision making from the aspect of selling ourselves and our products or ideas to people we know or have had an opportunity to "size up" so to speak. There is another side of the coin, however, those people we have just met, as in an interview. Success in business ventures and projects often hinges on our ability to choose the right person, i.e., make decisions about individuals based on limited information. We can enhance our ability to size up people we have just met or have limited information about by becoming more sensitive to our intuition - our gut feeling.

People who have a reputation of making fairly accurate assessments of others have usually learned to tune in to this sense. It is a matchless guide when properly used however this sense or skill is also highly susceptible to distortion and interference from other elements of the personality. For example, emotional biases, emotional problems, predispositions and prejudices, and excessive rationality can cloud or block out dependable feedback from intuition.

There is also the problem of making the proper distinction between intuition and prejudice. Intuition works by picking up perceptions that come to us from cues and bits and pieces of information so small and subtle they aren't detected by our conscious observation process. Intuition we can say, is the voice of our spirit man. Therefore, the intuition is most dependable and useful when registering information about someone we have just met. On the other hand, prejudice, or prejudgment, comes from predisposed thinking based on teaching or experiences with someone of similar characteristics.

To hone your intuitive skills, check first impressions - don't rely on gut feelings alone. Take precautions and validate by making a rational assessment of the facts presented to you. Do the facts bear out and does what the person says and does jive with your impressions? Look for contradictions between words, tone, and body language. If all systems say go, follow your intuition. If not, backtrack and try to find what things are not in harmony.

You must also check yourself. Review the track record of your ability to judge accurately and you may get some indication of a bias in your decisions. For example, you may be attracted to persons with your personality or background, or you may have a particular aversion toward articulate individuals which causes you to ignore your intuitive sense.

Finally, avoid using gut feelings in your decision making process if you are in a stressed or emotional state. These states definitely cloud or block dependable feedback from intuition.

Continuous Improvement

Too many people place the responsibility for their lives and careers in the hands of the organization where they work, and depend on an organization to help organize their lives and decide what's best for them. This should not be the case. The Reverend Robert Schuller wrote a book entitled, *If It's Going To Be, It's Up To Me.* To apply the title to this situation, it is your life, your goals, and your career and you must be the one to initiate and follow through on the actions needed to accomplish your mission.

Another reason you should take a more proactive approach is that at least one study has suggested that employer-sponsored training has a racial bias. A study, *Who Receives Formal Firm Sponsored Training in the U.S.*? by Craig Olson, School of Business and Industrial Relations Research Institute, University of Wisconsin-Madison, revised July, 1996, concluded the following, "Depending on the definition of employer sponsorship, whites were 45 percent (at work) to 70 percent (time off) more likely to receive employer sponsored training than were non-white workers."

Even in organizations that offer career development, there is inconsistency and some instability because of constant change. No organization can or will guarantee even if you are part of a development process that your career will move steadily up the ladder. Nor can you take for granted that how you are developing today in the organization will be relevant to your career tomorrow. Peter Drucker, considered to be the father of modern management, had this to say, "Progressive companies need to make continuous learning part of every job......Because knowledge is constantly changing, it demands continual learning. Skills should be refined and retooled every few years."

It has been theorized that 90 percent of the knowledge available in the Year 2000 did only come into awareness after the Year 1970. That's a mind - blowing estimate. Therefore, professional and technical obsolescence can easily occur in a rapidly changing environment such as we operate and should not be left to chance or to the organization's management. You must stay abreast of the latest developments in your field and do this on your own by requesting internal and external training, even if you have to fund your own way to a training that you think will enhance your career progress. Other ways to keep abreast are:

- Follow social, political, economic and technological trends to see where the world is going.
- Embrace and learn new technology ahead of the masses.
- Stay plugged into the youth market. This will help you be aware of the changing values in society.
- Read. Read. Read.

Managing Change

Charles F. Kettering was quoted to have said, "We must all be concerned with the future because we will have to spend the rest of our lives there." And one certain thing about the future is change will occur, and to be successful in life that fact must be accepted. Anything that does not change is dying or already dead. In order to deal effectively with change we need to do three things:

1. **Recognize** that we live in a dynamic environment and learn to anticipate and embrace change.
2. **Review** the impact of the change or potential change on our environment.
3. **Respond** with a plan of action that maximizes our opportunities and minimizes the threats to our surroundings and us.

The first step is to recognize change. Change can be categorized as incremental or transformational. Transformational change is a lot easier to recognize but perhaps the more challenging of the two to set a strategy for. It is like going from horse-driven to internal combustion engine-driven carriages, or from central computer driven processing to personal computer driven processing. Existing systems and processes will not work well or at all any more.

On the other hand, incremental change is somewhat more difficult to recognize, many times because we are an integral part of the process. It's like the old saying of not being able to see the forest for the trees. It may thus be the more menacing of the two. Incremental change is depicted in the story of the frog. The frog is a cold-blooded animal whose temperature changes with the environment. So the story goes, if a frog is put in a pot of hot water it immediately tries to jump out because it recognizes the discomfort from such a large and immediate change in its environment. However, if it is put in a pot of water close to its body temperature and the water temperature is gradually increased, it will die, not recognizing the danger of the slowly elevating temperature.

The same incremental process happens in our society. Since incremental changes usually occur gradually and over a period of time we often become desensitized to these changes in our surroundings and the subtleties that are taking place. However, we sooner or later realize we are in a different environment with different challenges and opportunities and we haven't adequately planned for the new. Both individuals and organizations become uncompetitive, irrelevant, and yes, sometimes die prematurely, as a result of this incremental change. Western Union is a good example of a company that succumbed to incremental change. It failed to stay abreast of the technological innovations and demographic changes affecting its business and today is a weak replica of what it could have been in this information age.

To recognize change, one must STOP, LOOK, & LISTEN to their surroundings often.

STOP.	Don't become complacent in your current environment.
LOOK.	Check the temperature around you often.
LISTEN.	Check the sources and sound levels around you often.

The second step in managing change effectively is to review and estimate the impact of a potential change on our environment. If we are to manage this stage effectively, we must be proactive and try to access the risks and rewards of the outcomes. To adequately estimate the impact, it is necessary to know the characteristics of change or the dynamics of change. Let's take transformational change as an example in describing this step. While incremental change is subtle, transformational change is bold. You know change has and is occurring, you're just not sure what or how to respond best to it.

Transformational change is usually caused by some tension or dissatisfaction with the status quo, as a result of changing values or visions, or is due to some technology breakthrough. A driving force must exist to agitate or to cause the tension or dissatisfaction. Therefore, to estimate the impact of transformational change, we must know the driving forces and their potential to change our environment. This allows us to position ourselves better for the opportunities and to lessen the impact of the threats. For example, today, one of the main driving forces causing transformational changes in our communications and electronic industries is the speed and power of technology development, especially digital technology.

There is usually one or more opposing or restraining forces resisting the change, just as there may be more than one driving force pushing the change. These restraining forces are like inertia in an inanimate object that resist motion once it has come to rest. We must know the restraining forces and their potential as well.

The third and final step in managing change is to fashion a correct, or at least a good response that consists of at least three elements. First is the recognition that in order to grow, to survive, or just to maintain against the driving forces of change, some experimentation and risk taking is necessary in our response to the potential rewards and risks.

The second element in developing a good response or plan to deal with change is to control one of the biggest restraining forces to change - FEAR. I talked about fear earlier under decision making. One of the main reasons we as humans resist change is to maintain the comfort level of the known and avoid or postpone the discomfort level resulting from the unknown - the confusion, ambiguity, and frustration that comes with change. Therefore, to begin effectively to control the negative effects of fear, one must accept the truth that change is inevitable. It is the process of a living organism. All growth is change but all change is not growth. Focusing your energy to create personal growth with the change helps control the fear.

The third element in fashioning an effective plan is to accept the fact that when the driving forces and restraining forces collide, either could prevail. There will be some uncertainty but regardless of the outcome, we must be committed to the process - to the seeking of the best outcome. If the restraining forces prevail, we go back to the status quo but usually only for a while. As the driving forces get stronger, they will eventually break through, creating a new situation. Those who have anticipated and prepared for change find it easier to redefine, reframe, and reshape their existing environment to accommodate the change. Over a period of time, they become competent and master the change, and not only survive, but also thrive in the new situation.

Career success requires you to remember that there will always be driving forces for change and, therefore, the need to change. The process is continuous. With the increased emphasis in the corporate world on the bottom line, people who are likely to be the most successful are those who possess the experience needed to become quickly functional in a changing atmosphere and make contributions that can impact the organization. Therefore, the key words for your success in a changing environment are **awareness** and **adaptability**. Don't forget the frog that succumbed to incremental change because it was not aware. However, the individual or organization that is killed by transformational change (usually because they lacked adaptability) is just as dead.

Being a Team Player

When Magic Johnson first came into the NBA with the Los Angeles Lakers in the 1970s, he played all five positions during one playoff game. To my knowledge no one else in the NBA had, or has ever done this. The feat that Magic accomplished in this game epitomizes the two basic ingredients a player needs to contribute to the success of a team, knowledge and skills. He had a thorough knowledge of the purpose of the game, knowledge of the goals being sought, and knowledge of the roles and responsibilities of each position on the team. And not only did he have the knowledge, he also had the skills to perform the roles and responsibilities of each position extremely well.

When it comes to the teams we participate with, we should have the knowledge that allows us to understand, support and feel ownership of the team's purpose and goal. While we may not have the flexibility in skills of Magic, we should have the specific skills to perform our roles and responsibilities and the general skills to forge the interdependent relations with other members that maximizes productivity of the unit.

With that background, here are some characteristics of a good team player:

1. A willingness to put the team's goals and objectives first. The team player understands that the team's goals and his/her personal goals must be one in order to produce a win-win environment for all.

2. A good listener. The team player is an active listener, that is, s/he pays attention to the other person's total communications process - the words, the tone and the body language. S/he gives feedback by clarifying and rephrasing what the speaker has said which minimizes misinterpretation and lessens or avoids prejudgment.

3. Both "task" and "team" focused. The team player recognizes the importance of working through the dynamics of the team process while yet accomplishing the tasks that must be completed. The process includes managing conflict, reaching a method on decision-making (majority, consensus, etc) and other relational issues.

4. Communicates openly and honestly. The team player is assertive enough to voice an honest opinion and present his/her case in a way that does not affect the harmony of the group even though s/he may be the only one with the divergent view. S/he works to resolve conflict when it surfaces.

5. Builds trust and mutual respect. The effective team player knows how to build trust by being self-disclosing and communicating openly and honestly. If s/he senses a lack of trust in the relationship, a conscious choice is made to do something to bridge the gap.

6. Respects differences and values diversity. The team player puts time and effort in understanding the similarities, and most especially, recognizing the differences in the team members that allow them to analyze and view the same things differently. S/he recognizes the backgrounds, experiences and personalities of the members have created a uniqueness that allows them to make special contributions and enhance the results of the team.

Chapter 8

Making the Most of a Slight Edge

You've read about the career influence factors and the sources of personal positive influence that distinguish the "chosen" from the "also ran". Yet another way to add value to yourself is to develop and make the most of a slight edge because in today's environment, one needs every advantage. Corporations are harnessing technology to produce more goods and services with far fewer employees. In 1982, the S&P 500 companies employed 15 million people. Today, they employ less than 10 million while sales and profits have doubled, thanks to technology.

There are two basic strategies for progress in any human activity: (1) striving for the big breakthrough, i.e., going for broke; or (2) playing for small increases that eventually add up. There are some noteworthy cases where the first approach proved successful, but generally in life, sports and in business, it is safe to say that the most success has come from achieving a series of small advantages. Some baseball games are won dramatically by late inning home runs, but most of the time the outcome depends on putting together singles, bunts, walks and sacrifice flies. Most of the time the football team that wins has the most first downs. Therefore, the latter strategy is likely to be appropriate and successful when long-range goals are being sought, as in your career, and when circumstances allow for graduated efforts, so focus on playing for small increases.

Personal growth is a matter of small increments. All athletes know this so they work hard at developing the slight edge. The prizefighter and the defensive lineman both know that if their reflexes can be an eye blink quicker than the opponent, it can mean the difference between success and failure.

The same is true in developing a successful career. That is why it is so important to study yourself, your competition, and your environment to see how you may be able to develop a slight edge. Following are two techniques that can help you toward this end:

1. Developing and exercising creativity in your work and lifestyle and;

2. Using visualization (with optimism) of your success.

The first technique that can help you to develop an edge is to learn how to unleash your creative abilities. Motivational experts indicate that adopting new thought processes does not mean being falsely optimistic or grandiose. Nor does it mean to deny discouragement. It is mental capacity to seek and find workable, beneficial solutions, displaying a positive mental attitude. It involves dealing constructively with problems and requires the use of goals and action plans. Dr. Ramon J. Aldag, University of Wisconsin's chair of the business school's Department of Management and Human Resources stated the following during an interview recorded with UW Business Update magazine in the December, 1997 edition;

> "Everything going on in the business environment is putting a premium on creativity. The new world of work and organizations is a place of complexity, ambiguity, change, diversity, and globalization. In this environment , creativity and flexibility often become more important than choice making and efficiency. Companies must develop creative responses to external competitive, legal, and technological imperatives, as well as internal challenges such as reorganizing, empowering employees, or dealing with sexual harassment."

The emphasis almost everywhere in business now is on the most cost-effective ways of doing things. This kind of atmosphere presents an outstanding opportunity for you to stand out among peers and get the notice and attention of decision makers and influentials in your organization (gain distinction). If early on in your career or new position you can come up with ideas and solutions, and participate in implementing them that saves the company money or strengthens its competitive position you will gain distinction.

Furthermore, in dealing with ongoing issues and concerns, or solving complex problems within a sphere of influence, the person who can come up with creative, workable solutions will usually be sought out for his/her input or participation. And this participation can provide the edge needed for advancement – the career track. Therefore, one must work to enhance his/her creativity and here are a few techniques:

1. Focus on being creative. Set aside 30-60 minutes per day of quiet time to develop creative solutions within your sphere of influence. Concentrate on one situation at a time.
2. Learn to be a careful observer of your surroundings. By doing this you can often notice details ignored or overlooked by others.
3. Use the following acronym, CREATE, to challenge and stimulate your conscious mind about the situation, problem, challenge or assignment:

Combine. Can improvements be made or the problem be solved by linking existing familiar functions that have been dissociated in the past?

Rearrange. Can improvements be made or the problem be solved by changing the sequence or order of the existing system or method?

Extend or **E**xaggerate. Can improvements be made or the problem be solved by extending the form or function of the existing?

Add. Can a new element be added to an existing element to improve its performance.

Transfer, **T**ake away. Can something be removed from the existing and placed with something else?

Eliminate. Can something be eliminated entirely? Is it no longer necessary? Is it redundant?

4. Once you have gone through the conscious exercise in Step 3, you will increase your chances of obtaining a creative solution within the conscious realm of thinking and reasoning. However, the real breakthrough will come when your subconscious mind starts to process this information, and solutions will pop into your mind when you are not even thinking of the situation.

Furthermore, you can get greater insights about your own strengths and weaknesses, better understand co-workers, and better understand the organization you work for by understanding creativity styles. This insight will help you to see your patterns and preferences in idea generation, the types of ideas you are likely to generate, the types of solutions you are likely to accept, and effective ways to communicate your ideas.

There are many tools that can help you identify your creativity style, and one such tool I like is the Kirton Adaptation-Innovation (KAI) Theory. It is based on an X-Y scale that determines if a person is more adaptive or innovative in their creative thinking to solve problems and make decisions. Both styles are creative but channel their creativity in different ways.

To briefly describe, the KAI scale ranges from 32 as most adaptive to 160 as most innovative. This range is further subdivided into originality, efficiency, and rule conformity. A lower score on originality suggests one tends to produce fewer original ideas, but these ideas are more likely to be viewed as useful or relevant. A higher score suggests one tends to produce more original ideas, but they are less likely to be accepted immediately. A lower score on efficiency suggests you prefer being thorough and efficient in handling tasks, and a higher score means the opposite. On rule conformity, those on the lower end prefer to operate within rules and structure, while those on the higher end are less constrained.

Those individuals who score in the adapters category are said to be: predictable; good managers of time and money; comprehensive planners; good at applying structure to innovative ideas; creative in productive ways; cautious risk-takers; and hesitant to "rock the boat."

Innovators are seen as flexible, unrestrained by limited resources, enthusiastic, breakers of new ground, productive in creative ways, but are capricious risk-takers, and viewed as arrogant and wanting change just for the sake of change.

In a team environment, adapters influence the team with innovators by supplying stability, order, and continuity. They maintain group cohesion and cooperation and are generally sensitive to others. They provide a safety net for riskier operations.

Innovators influence the adapters by breaking with accepted past theories and provide the dynamics to bring about radical change. However, they can often threaten group cohesion and cooperation and are generally less sensitive to others who have a different style.

I hope this protracted discussion on techniques of creativity and tools for identifying creativity styles will stimulate you to further improve your skills in this area by doing more study. Greater knowledge can mean a greater edge.

The second technique for helping you develop an edge has to do with mental rehearsal. What does it take to be the top or best, or even be among the top or best at what you do? It takes drive, ambition, skill, dedication and hard work. But these aren't the only things. There is one technique that can give you a slight edge, has been proven to work, and is found right inside your head. In fact, it is the power of your own thought processes. As simple and nonscientific as it may sound, the way you think has been shown in empirical, sophisticated research to separate the champions from the also-rans. As a motivational technique, it is called mental rehearsal, skull practice or simply, visualization.

A great deal of study has focused on the psychology of visualization - the planning, evaluating, troubleshooting, and envisioning success through your mind before the big event. Experts from the various fields of physiology, nutrition, biomechanics, podiatry, psychology, and medicine have studied mental practice, goal setting, visualization, and imagery.

There is general agreement that it does have a positive benefit. Researchers have found that successful people have a distinctive style, a permanence or consistency in their thinking, which they apply generously in both physical and mental rehearsal. Moreover, those persons who are fatalists and seem helpless against the world also use a permanent, consistent mental rehearsal that hampers their progress.

Dr. Martin E.P. Seligman, an expert in the field, did pioneering research beginning back in the 1970s. Dr. Seligman completed several studies in sales and sports to measure the impact of optimism when combined with mental rehearsal. His research in sales indicated those whose mental rehearsal was pessimistic sold considerably less, while the optimistic individuals worked longer and sold more. The pessimistic tended to drop out of the training program at a higher rate.

Among a group of U.S. Olympic team swimmers, a similar test was conducted. The swimmers were asked to swim as fast as they could and at the end of the heat were told that they did not swim as fast as they had expected to. They were told to rest and visualize their performance in an Olympic match. Those who had previously tested as optimistic thinkers got faster, the pessimistic thinkers got slower. The latter performances had nothing to do with their talent, they were all talented, instead, the results had a lot to do with how positive their mental rehearsals were.

The point is a simple one as these studies indicate. The individual who has a plan with specific goals, objectives and actions that combines optimism with his/her visualization of success can achieve a greater measure of success - can develop an edge. With this key point in mind, following are some suggestions by the experts to perfect the techniques of visualization:

1. Be accurate in your rehearsal. Work out a step-by-step sequence of events and write them down. Read and rehearse the behavior or event daily until it becomes habit. Where proper technique is involved, be sure you picture it properly. Only perfect practice makes perfect. Otherwise, practice just makes permanent.

2. Give yourself positive feedback as you rehearse daily.

3. Coach yourself mentally with the truth. Dr. Seligman's research suggests that optimistic, successful people believe three things: most problems are temporary; one defeat does not spell failure in all areas; and you have more control than you may think.

4. Be consistently optimistic. It may be difficult at first until you break old mindsets of "can't do".

5. Select the right time of day if it is a physical activity and try to do your visualization during the same time as the event would take place. Otherwise, get into a relaxed state and picture yourself doing the job, task, event or presentation and doing it well. Try to make the image as visible as possible so you can really feel the self-confidence that goes along with the job or position or task.

6. Finally, stick with it. Mentally it cost you nothing to give the greatest presentation, or write the best software package, or be the top salesperson, or run thc biggest corporation. I once heard a preacher say if you fall among the stars you are still on high ground.

Chapter 9

Conclusion: Managing the Process for Attaining Maximum Personal Results

We are all looking for results; from our employer, our employees, our spouses, our children, and our friends. Results come through a process of identifying and effectively and efficiently managing the key variables that influence our environment. Management theory says that managers achieve results in their areas of responsibility by planning, organizing, leading, motivating, and controlling. We all have to manage these functions in our daily lives if we want to get and stay on the career track.

The challenge in today's complex and competitive society is to integrate these as personal skills into a framework that allows us effectively to process a myriad of information and balance competing agendas in order to make the right choices that attain the desired results. In essence, the challenge is to achieve the end, the career goal, while enjoying the journey or pursuit of it. This can only be done through the maintenance of a balanced lifestyle that allows quality time for health, family, social, spiritual, and intellectual development.

The theories and principles to help you attain greater personal results in your career pursuits have been discussed throughout the book and are summarized as follows:

- Learn the system
- Develop and hone the necessary skills
- Develop and maintain a positive mental attitude
- Make a good plan
- Set priorities
- Pace yourself daily

Once you have determined where you are by using the assessment tools provided to you in this book and have decided on a course of action whether it is plight, fight or flight, "go for the gusto." Develop and maintain a positive attitude. Empirical evidence continues to mount that shows people who have a positive attitude live longer, happier lives and are more successful.

Develop a written plan because a plan defines purpose and establishes direction. The old saying, "If you don't know where you are going, all roads lead there," is certainly true. Again, research shows organizations and people who develop and follow written plans have a greater probability of achieving their plans.

Set priorities. After making a plan and identifying the resources needed to accomplish the plan, you will find that you probably don't have all the resources currently at your disposal to complete the plan. You will have to set some priorities regarding the order in which you want to do things.

Priorities are needed for both the short term and long term.

Regardless if a person sets his/her priorities consciously or unconsciously, they are based on an underlying value system. You should develop the habit of thinking about your values and setting the proper priorities on a conscious basis using the tools provided herein.

Lastly, pace yourself. Pacing connotes taking the appropriate actions at the appropriate time as outlined in your plan, which covers a long-term view, while maintaining a balanced lifestyle. Because the world's situation is changing so rapidly, many people, in order to keep up, live their lives as if they are in a 100 - meter race rather than a marathon. However, this is neither healthy nor wise.

Pacing requires separating the urgent from the important. Urgency is a time matter. Importance is a consequence or outcome matter involving the magnitude of the outcome of the results that will follow. For example, we usually have a sense of urgency to answer our phone. It may or may not be important. Or, it may be important to your career goals to get an MBA. The urgency depends on the timetable you and /or your organization have imposed.

Pacing also requires the skills to choose between efficiency and effectiveness. Efficiency is "doing thing right" while effectiveness is "doing the right things." There are times when one is more important than the other.

In conclusion, regardless of whether you are on a career track or a side track, maximizing your personal results is a laudable pursuit and I believe the theories and principles discussed in this book will help. I'll end with a quote that I read long ago. It has helped me to maintain a positive attitude in pursuit of my goals and dreams. "Success is getting up one more time than you fall down." I bid you "God speed" in your pursuit of the career track.

Appendix A

Personal Values Clarification

1. Carefully review your personal values from the following list. Add others that are important to you.
2. Rate each one by placing a check mark in the appropiate column; "H" means High, "M" means Medium, and "L" means Low.
3. Choose the five highest and rank from one to five in the last column.

Values	Rating			Ranking
	H	M	L	Top Five
Loyalty (To one's responsibilities and commitments)				
Dependability / Reliability				
Integrity (Honesty, true to beliefs)				
Self-respect (Personal worth and value)				
Inner Harmony (Peace, contentment)				
Order (Stability and predictability in life)				
Openness (Ability to be self-disclosing)				
Affection (Love, caring for self and others)				
Nurturance (Loving development)				
Involvement (Belonging and participating)				
Happiness				
Support (Encouragement and assistance)				
Helpfulness (In assisting others)				
Comfort (Being at ease with surroundings)				
Independence (Freedom to act and do)				
Perseverance				
Financial Independence				
Spiritual Harmony (with God and mankind)				
Intellectual Development				
Social Interaction (with friends and associates)				
Physical Health				
Safety and Security				

Appendix B

Work Values Clarification

1. Carefully review your work values from the following list. Add others that are important to you.
2. Rate each one by placing a check mark in the appropiate column; "H" means High, "M" means Medium, and "L" means Low.
3. Choose the five highest and rank from one to five in the last column.

Values	Rating			Ranking
	H	M	L	Top five
Recognition (Appreciation, respect from others)				
Achievement (A sense of accomplishment)				
Pay and Benefits				
Advancement (Promotion opportunities)				
Leadership (Control of other employees)				
Power (To affect change and make things happen)				
Feedback (On performance and work issues)				
Open Communications				
Responsibility (Clear delineation of work)				
Authority (The appropriate freedom to act)				
Accountability (Clear consequences for results)				
Autonomy (Freedom to make decisions)				
Creativity (Opportunity to be innovative)				
Utilization (Effective use of your skills)				
Development and Training Opportunities				
Satisfaction (Enjoy what you do)				
Inclusion (Feeling like a member of the team)				
Job Security				
Equal Opportunity and Fairness				
Aesthetic Surroundings (Work space, furnishings, fixtures)				
Pleasant Work Atmosphere (Attitudes and Stress Levels)				
Progressive Management				

Appendix C

The Personal Planning Process

I. Goals: (Long range - An ultimate achievement over a 10-20 year period, or over a lifetime.)

A. FINANCIAL (career, profession, investments)
Example: Become president of a company

B. FAMILY
Example: Maintain a good family life

C. SOCIAL
Example: Develop and maintain several meaningful friendships

D. SPIRITUAL
Example: Develop greater faith

E. HEALTH
Example: Maintain good health

F. Intellectual
Example: Visit six of the continents

II. GOALS OR OBJECTIVES: (Intermediate term, three to five year period)

A. FINANCIAL
Example: Be a division manager

B. FAMILY
Example: Spend more time with wife and children

C. SOCIAL
Example: Develop new friends

D. SPIRITUAL
Example: Become a leader in a local church

E. HEALTH
Example: Control hypertension

F. Intellectual
Example: Visit Africa and South America

III. PRIORITIES (In the order you will pursue)

A. Health

B. Family

C. Spiritual

D. Financial

E. Intellectual

F. Social

IV. OBJECTIVES: (Short term, one year or less)

Specific
Measurable
Attainable
Relevant
Time encompassed
(Emphasis should be on the highest priority items, therefore your personal resources, i.e., your money, talents, and time should be allocated accordingly.)

A. Health
Example: Control B/P to 120/80
Control weight below 185 pounds

B. Family

C. Spiritual

D. Financial

E. Intellectual

F. Social

V. Action Plans or Activities for Each Objective

A. Health

1. Add no salt to food after it is cooked.

2. Jog for 2.5 miles at least three times per week.

3. Eat sweets on only three days per week.

B. Family

C. Spiritual

D. Financial

E. Intellectual

F. Social